D0611820

The Search For Community

Other titles by George Melnyk

Of The Spirit: The Writings of Douglas Cardinal

Radical Regionalism

The Search
For Community

From Utopia to a Co-operative Society

George Melnyk

Montréal·Buffalo

HX626, M45 1985   c.2

Copyright © 1985 by George R. Melnyk
No part of this book may be reproduced or transmitted in any form by
means, electronic or mechanical, including photocopying and recording,
or by any information storage or retreival system, without written per-
mission from the author or publisher, except for brief passages quoted
by a reviewer in a newspaper or magazine.

Black Rose Books No. N96
ISBN Hardcover 0-920057-53-5
ISBN Paperback 0-920057-52-7

Canadian Cataloguing in Publication Data

Melnyk, George
    The Search for community: from Utopia to a co-operative
society

Includes index.
ISBN 0-920057-53-5 (bound). ISBN 0-920057-52-7 (pbk.).

1. Cooperation. 2. Cooperative societies.
I. Title.

HX626.M34 1985   334   C85-090201-0

Cover design: J.W. Stewart

Black Rose Books

3981 boul. St. Laurent   University of Toronto Press
Montréal, Québec   33 East Tupper St.
H2W 1Y5   Buffalo, New York 14230
Canada   USA

Typeset in Palacio by Pièce de Resistance Graphics, Edmonton
Printed and bound in Québec, Canada

To the Memory of E.A. Partridge
Father of the Co-operative Movement in Western Canada

CONTENTS

ACKNOWLEDGEMENTS

There are many people who helped make this book possible. In the early stages George Woodcock was most encouraging, as was Dr. Henri Desroche of the Centre de Recherches Cooperatifs in Paris. My colleagues at the Confederation of Alberta Faculty Association were supportive of my research while I was Executive Director from 1982 to 1984 and I thank them for granting me time from my official duties to pursue this topic.

A number of scholars have been kind enough to read the manuscript and offer their observations. In particular I wish to thank Dr. Ian Mac-Pherson, Chairman of the Department of History at the University of Victoria, for his unfailing interest and guidance throughout the writing process. Dr. J.R. Blasi of the Center for Jewish Studies at Harvard University provided useful comments on Chapter Four. Dr. Charles Erasmus of the Department of Anthropology, University of California at Santa Barbara, was kind enough to read Chapter Five. Dr. Jack Quarter of the Ontario Institute for Studies in Education provided me with insights into Chapters Six and Seven. Dr. Hayden Roberts of the Faculty of Extension, University of Alberta, helped clarify Chapter Eight. Mr. Laird Hunter of the Co-operative Union of Canada's Worker Co-op Project read a substantial part of the manuscript and offered useful advice. Their co-operation has helped eliminate errors in the early drafts. Whatever problems remain are of my own creation.

I wish to thank Lynn Hanley of Communitas Inc. for providing me with facilities where I could write the book in a congenial atmosphere, and Lesley Conley, the librarian at Communitas, for initiating me into the mysteries of writing on a computer. Alberta Culture's Film and Literary Arts helped financially with an Advanced Author's Grant in 1984. And my wife Julia assisted with her expert editorial comments and her encouragement.

PREFACE

My first reason for writing this book is an interest in co-ops. That interest began during my childhood in Winnipeg, when my parents took out a mortgage at a credit union. As immigrants they naturally turned to their own ethnic community's financial institutions when a major purchase was involved. Parental discussions of credit union affairs were my introduction to co-operative institutions.

But my first direct involvement did not come until I was a student in Toronto. I helped set up a food co-op in the Cabbagetown district when it was a poor neighbourhood. Although the food co-op was not all that successful, it was a small and friendly place where we had a good time making granola, the co-op's hottest selling item.

After settling in Edmonton I made a film about Keegano, the city's first housing co-op. Although I was not directly involved in co-ops, the co-operative reality was never far away. My first office was located at Communitas, a nonprofit agency for the development of co-op housing. It was here that I met a group of people with a strong commitment to co-op living. (A decade later Edmonton has a flourishing co-op sector with fifteen co-ops in operation and another dozen in the works. Much of the credit for this development belongs to the people of Communitas Inc.)

As a city person my primary connection with co-operatives has been as a consumer of financial services. That includes a mortgage with the credit union, insurance with Co-operators, and an RRSP with Co-op Trust. I suspect that represents the average level of involvement of those urban Canadians who deal with co-ops. It is not particularly activist. Yet my interest in the co-op ideal has led me to seek further involvement. When a study group on the idea of worker co-ops was started, I promptly joined. This was in the spring of 1984—the same time that I returned to Communitas to begin writing this book.

Besides the motivation that comes from a general interest in co-ops, there is also my urban working class identity. As the son of a factory worker, I have been concerned with the problems of labour. From the desk where I have been writing this book I look out onto a steel fabricating plant several hundred metres away. That plant symbolizes my urban industrial identity. But cities are not simply concrete and steel. They are also parks and rivers, gardens and woods. So in this book the reader will find the urban perspective with its dual attachment to the machine and to nature. The human component of the urban economy is the worker. My family experience in Winnipeg's industrial life has moulded my view of social justice. When I reflect on my parents' working life, I imagine how much better it could have been if the factories they worked in had been co-operatively owned and managed by the employees.

In addressing the issues facing workers one addresses the issues facing the majority of Western Canadians.[1] In the Eighties these issues are high unemployment and a decline in real income. When this is coupled with cutbacks in social services and erosion of the benefits provided by the welfare state, we can honestly say that the situation of workers has deteriorated significantly and in some cases has become desperate.[2] This book was written in response to these conditions.

My third reason for doing this book is my personal search for community. As the world becomes increasingly urbanized and industrialized, traditional community relations suffer. Martin Buber, the humanist philosopher, claimed that "the primary aspiration of all history is a genuine community of human beings."[3] As we approach the next century that aspiration becomes more pressing. Perhaps it is my lifelong experience of urban life that makes me sensitve to manageable sizes, closer interpersonal relations, and small communities. Or perhaps it is my memory of the 'Sixties generation' when youthful communalism was in vogue. Whatever its source, the personal need for sharing and supportive relations is accentuated by the competitive rush of mass society.

A commitment to regionalism and to Western Canada is the fourth motivation behind this book. Because of their history of fighting exploitation, I have a belief in the people of the region and their capacity to innovate populist solutions to social problems.[4] In the rural areas much was accomplished, but the weak industrial base of the region has meant that historically the workers did not have the same clout as farmers did.[5] But the economic and social problems of the region are serious enough today to encourage workers to develop new and radical solutions.

But why turn to the co-operative ideal for answers when the region's co-ops seem in the words of one report, "largely isolated from contemporary sources of innovation, challenge, and ferment? People do not see co-operatives as relevant to social change."[6] The report points out that millions of Canadians belong to co-operatives but few are active or informed. For the great majority of co-operators the movement has been supplanted by a system. What the authors of the report suggest is that the co-operative reality in Canada must be rejuvenated through a new vision. That is precisely what this book attempts to do. It presents a vision of a new kind of co-operative which is meant to deal specifically with the social and economic problems of the present period.

A knowledge of the history of co-operation is basic to any new formulation of the co-operative ideal. That is why the first part of this book provides a comprehensive review of co-operative and collectivist models from around the world. These models are analyzed to see whether any part of them can be adapted to Western Canada.

The second part of the book goes on to propose a new form of co-operative community called a 'social co-operative.' The name has been chosen to express the social goals of the co-op and to distinguish it from producer, consumer, and worker co-ops. The concept of social co-ops draws on the achievements of the world-wide co-operative movement for its basic structure, principles of operation, and goals. While firmly rooted in the Western Canadian experience, social co-ops are applicable on a national basis because the region shares many problems with the rest of Canada. Nevertheless, the concept of social co-ops is meant to address specifically the historic needs of the region for economic diversification and industrialization as well as providing a way of dealing with the immediate need for employment and social services.

This book is dedicated to the memory of E. A. Partridge, the founder of the United Grain Growers and the father of the co-operative movement in Western Canada. He, along with thousands of other Prairie farmers, pioneered the co-operative way as an answer to corporate exploitation. May his spirit and those who joined him guide this book.

George R. Melnyk
Edmonton, Alberta
April 18, 1985

Part One:
THE HISTORICAL TRADITION

Chapter One:
AN INTRODUCTION

A DEFINITION

The word 'co-operative' is ordinarily associated with the consumer co-operative store established in 1844 at Rochdale, England, by a group of twenty-eight people who have come to be known as the Rochdale Pioneers. Yet the term 'co-operative' was one of many words used to describe collective self-help. In the nineteenth century terms such as associationist, communalist, communist, harmonist, mutualist, and socialist were also used.[1] This variety reflected the fluid state of the co-operative concept early in its life.

What made Rochdale special is that it worked and became the basis for a worldwide movement. A Canadian historian of the movement says that Rochdale "provided the rules by which co-operative societies could function; but they were also very adaptable and could be utilized by all classes, all shades of political opinion, and all nations."[2] These rules have now been condensed into the following six principles: voluntary and open membership, democratic control, limited return on capital, surplus earnings belong to the members, member education and co-operation among co-operatives.[3]

It is the organizational flexibility of these principles that is the cornerstone of co-operative development. "Co-operation has taken a great variety of forms," says the Canadian co-operator G. Davidovic, "from loose associations such as Italian fishermen co-operatives for administering member insurance...to rigidly organized and cohesive Israeli kibbutzim with community ownership, work, and life. And between these two extremes there is a large range of co-operative types..."[4] Since co-operation has found institutional expression in everything from banking to utopian communities, one has to take a broad view in order to understand the co-operative concept and its development. It has been the principle

3

used to provide child care, to build houses, to farm land, and even to bury people. Sometimes it dealt with only a small part of a person's life, while at other times it has been all encompassing.

"A co-operative is an organization created for the practice of co-operation," is a definition that may sound circular but is actually helpful.[5] It captures the intent of people grouping together to help themselves. Davidovic makes it equally succinct when he defines co-operation as "a social movement based on self-help."[6]. The distribution of benefits deriving from the act of co-operation and the democratic manner in which the co-operation is managed finds different expressions in different cultures and in different historical periods. Whenever people create institutions based on principles that are open to interpretation, these institutions will have a wide spectrum of characteristics.

The debate over the nature of co-operatives reflects this wide range of co-operative reality. The kibbutzim of Israel have been described as "the most extreme realization of the principle of co-operation."[7] While at the other end of the co-operative specturm is the view of Lazlo Valko, who states that "the collective form of living is contradictory to human nature." and that "the co-operative is a tool to bring economic and/or social welfare to the individual members, without dissolving their individuality in the colourless conglomerate of the collective."[8] He says this in spite of the fact that Rochdale was rooted in the utopian socialist ideas of Robert Owen, a British factory reformer and an advocate of communal living.[9] Using a wider interpretation of co-operation than Valko, Henri Desroche, one of the intellectual leaders of the co-operative movement in this century, accepts the Soviet collective farm—the kolkhoz—as a co-operative enterprise, in spite of the fact that it is a state-created entity.[10] If we define co-operation as people working together in a spirit of self-help and mutual aid for their common good, then we remain open to all the variations that have been created prior and subsequent to Rochdale.

The co-operative ideal and all the institutions it has spawned cannot be placed on a hierarchical scale with some higher and others lower. This approach would be blind to the reality of different cultures and it would result in a moralistic judgement based on one system alone. This would undermine the very flexibility and adaptability that has built co-operation. I prefer to place co-operatives on a horizontal continuum where they are equal. When Charles Gide, a former president of the International Co-operative Alliance and a leading co-operative thinker, wrote some time ago that "a co-operative society is really an association that may be at any point on the scale between individualism and communism." he was simply describing the fact that co-operatives are found in every political and economic system in the world.[11] They are found in systems that promote individual entrepreneurship and in systems that praise collective ownership. This international reality is a key feature of co-operation.

Co-operation has grown and expanded when it has been willing "to experiment with new formulations and novel approaches that go beyond the formal co-operative structure and the conservative wisdom regarding Rochdale principles."[12] That experimentation has resulted from the interaction of local conditions with people's knowledge of the way things are done in other places and by other people. Therefore, co-operation is a process of experimentation and cross-fertilization.

Not every co-operative or collective model that will be examined in this book complies with all the official co-operative principles that have been adopted by the International Co-operative Alliance. (Originally they could agree on four, which was half the ones spelled out in the initial Rochdale charter.) Yet every form of co-operation has a contribution to make to our understanding of co-operative development. By looking at the history of co-operation on a global basis we can learn how and why these particular kinds of organizational forms arose and how they were augmented and modified by historical circumstances. This in turn will assist us in understanding contemporary pressures and how they influence future co-operative development.

ROCHDALE AND BEYOND: An Introduction to Co-operative History

George Jacob Holyoake, a nineteenth century British writer on co-operation, located the origin of modern co-operative institutions in the ideas of European thinkers of the late eighteenth and early nineteenth century. He mentions the French utopian socialists St. Simon (1760-1825) and Charles Fourier (1772-1837) and the English industrialist Robert Owen (1771-1858) as important precursors of Rochdale.[13]

Holyoake's contemporary, Beatrice Potter (Mrs. Sidney Webb) was more chauvinistic when she claimed that "...the Co-operative movement was purely British in origin."[14] She considered the co-operative retail store established at Rochdale as the fountainhead of the consumer co-op movement, which was itself the pinnacle of co-operation in her eyes. But Holyoake's wider perspective is more valid because it takes into account continental European contributions to co-operation, such as the German co-operative society or credit union begun by F.W. Raiffeisen and Herman Schulze in the 1850s.

While acknowledging the centrality of the Rochdale model, the French scholar, Henri Desroche, states that "the Rochdale tradition inherited a pre-Rochdale associationism rooted in a long line of socialist experiments of both religious and secular kinds."[15] The role of utopian communities such as those established by Robert Owen in both England and the United States in the early nineteenth century (to be discussed in detail in Chapter 5) is evident in the fact that half of those who founded the Rochdale store were Owenite socialists.[16]

Rochdale was a watershed. It helps divide co-operative history into three distinct phases. The first phase is the pre-Rochdale or utopian phase, which can be dated from approximately 1800 to 1850. This was a time of experimentation, when a return to the small agrarian-style village community was considered the best answer to new capitalist industrialization. The second phase is the Rochdale or movement stage, when co-operative institutions took hold in a great variety of areas. It was a phase of spectacular expansion and establishment of the co-operative system. This period can be dated from 1850 to 1950 with the movement phase coming prior to 1900 in Europe and after 1900 in North America, while in the Third World it did not begin till after 1950. Quite rightly this can be considered the golden age of European-inspired Rochdale co-ops. The third stage is the post-Rochdale or systems stage in which we are presently living.[17] This stage is characterized by the end of the ideological fervor of the sort that existed during the proselytizing years of phase two. During that phase co-operatives were trying to win the world, while in phase three they are primarily concerned with managing their success. They now practice co-existence rather than conversion.[18] This nonideological approach has produced a reaction. From within the co-operative system there are calls for a return to the spirit of phase two—the movement phase.[19] From outside the co-op system, there are even more radical calls for a return to phase one—the stage of utopian communities.

The continuity that exists between each phase is evident in the elements that move from one phase to the other. For example, the goal of the Rochdale pioneers was utopian. They sought to create a self-supporting 'home colony.' Their society's articles included the construction of homes, manufacturing, farming, education, and even self-government.[20] When they became successful and copied they were no longer utopian.

This multi-functional approach viewed the retail stores as a first step. But the store became an end in itself when the Rochdale members went on to step two—a co-operatively-owned cotton mill, which they established in 1858, but which subsequently was privatized. The retail store idea grew in popularity and consumer co-ops became the norm. In the earlier utopian phase there had been no distinction between consumer and producer co-operatives because everything was part of a single co-operative organization. In the utopian phase what mattered was the whole, while in the movement stage it was the part that counted. When the Rochdale Pioneers incorporated the Rochdale Co-operative Manufacturing Society separately from the store, they began the process of separating co-operation into functional units. Likewise the world's first co-operative law—the Industrial and Provident Societies Act—passed by the British Parliament in 1852, encouraged a proliferation of unifunctional co-ops.[21] The fate of the cotton mill was sealed when it enrolled both workers and nonworker members and then subscribed nonworking shareholders, who quickly took over. When the mill was converted to an ordinary joint-stock company only fifty of the 500 employees were actually shareholders.[22]

The failure of co-operation in the productive process led Beatrice Potter to claim that the greatest achievement of British co-operation was the dividend on purchase.[23] She condemned the whole idea of industrial production co-ops (worker co-ops) as an idea that "originated in a foreign land."[24] Yet the idea was English and Rochdale enough, only it had failed in that particular instance.

The following figures provide an insight into the success of the Rochdale approach. Twenty years after the founding of Rochdale, the Manchester Wholesale Society was started in the industrial heartland of England to service retail co-op stores with 18,337 members. By 1877 it was serving 588 societies with 273,351 members. And forty years after its beginning it was serving 1,133 retail stores representing 1,445,099 members.[25]

Compartmentalization and specialization was a reflection of the evolution of industrial society. Co-operative stores were created by "the better-off and thriftier sections of the working class" to provide an answer to the exploitation and abuses of the capitalist system.[26] The new industrial proletariat became the largest class with poverty its predominant economic position. The worker turned to consumer co-ops to lower his cost of consumption and the trade union to increase his income. Traditional agrarian self-sufficiency made no sense in an industrial framework where specialization and the cash economy became the norm. Under the Rochdale system, the worker remained an individual consumer while he created a collectively-owned instrument of consumption. But he did not create a collectively-owned instrument of production. Instead, the farmer as a small unit of production turned to co-operatives for marketing. Areas like Eastern Europe had a large peasant population with small holdings that was attracted to co-ops. The same thing happened in North America when the West was settled. What the Rochdale rules allowed was the maintenance of individual consumption and production with group protection and power.

The widespread success of co-operative institutions resulted in the formation of the International Co-operative Alliance in 1895. By 1977 the ICA represented more than 600,000 co-ops in sixty-five countries with 355 million members.[27] The power of the Rochdale experiment is evident in the composition of the ICA which continues to be dominated by the European consumer co-ops. Second are the agricultural producer co-ops and finally the industrial co-operatives.[28]

The present systems phase in co-operation is restricted in its power to innovate. Its essential reality is to reproduce ever larger conglomerate forms. Only in the developing nations are grassroots co-ops spreading. Alexander Laidlaw described today's phase as an age of 'ideological crisis.'[29] What he meant is that the present leadership of the co-operative systems are a managerial class whose viewpoint is anti-ideological. What they consider 'ideological' is the idealism of the utopian phase.[30] The huge organizations which have come to dominate the co-operative movement generate administrators and consolidators of the status quo. However, the utopianism of co-operative ideals continues to exist into this present phase. The crisis of conscience that presently affects the system results from the continued survival of the ideals developed in the utopian phase, 150 years ago.

Co-operation developed historically as a constant tug of war between the ideal and the practical. It begins with a need that is answered by a variety of ideal solutions. Through a process of trial and error, a successful model emerges which discredits previous unsuccessful attempts. This model is then hailed as the realistic one for others to copy. As the realistic model proliferates it begins to lose touch with its utopian or idealistic roots. Yet the farther away it gets from those roots, the stronger the pressure grows to return to those ideals. So when a co-operative fails to fill a need, idealists found a new one and the process begins all over again.

This cycle operates on the micro-level for each co-operative and it exists on the macro level as the three stages of the Rochdale model. The present-day systems people expand a system quantitatively . But those who return to original beginnings and start anew reinvigorate the co-operative reality qualitatively. That is why beginning anew is so important for co-operation. At every new beginning there is a utopian phase in which ideals predominate and lend their strength. The constant return to ideals is part of the essential vitality of co-operation. When we look at that first stage of co-operative history—the utopian phase—we see that it is not something purely historical, but that it retains a presence today. Its contemporary role is to guard ideals. But it is the second stage—the pragmatic phase—that makes the whole process real and substantive.

If the co-operative movement had not become a system, it would never have progressed to the present stage of reappraisal.

The history of co-operation is not just a history of the mainstream; it is a history of schism, reaction, and failure. Without the spin-offs and deadends, co-operation would not have developed. And it is development that is crucial to any living thing. When we combine this emphasis on the evolutionary nature of co-operative history with a broad definition of what constitutes co-operation we have the basis on which to view and classify co-operatives in a way which respects cultural, social, and political differences while retaining core co-operative ideals. The result is a fourfold tradition, which has gone through a utopian-movement-systems cycle.

THE FOUR HISTORICAL TRADITIONS

The way one chooses to compare co-operatives depends on the goals one has. For example, if one wishes to compare the economic performance of a variety of producer co-ops one can compare them on the basis of the economic areas in which they operate. If one wants to compare the full range of co-operative forms that have existed during the past 150 years, one must adopt a system of classification that is both simple and yet far-reaching in scope. This is precisely what the theory of the four historical traditions does. The theory divides co-ops into four distinct political categories: liberal democratic, Marxist, socialist, and communalist. This fourfold division is simple yet it covers a global range of political economies. Admittedly, the use of political designations may be controversial to some, but there are good reasons for using them.

First, these four categories are those most often used by co-ops themselves. For example, the kibbutzim of Israel view themselves as islands of socialism, while communes in China present themselves as fulfillments of Marxist-Leninism. These ideological terms are the very terms which co-ops use to interpret themselves to their own society. By using these terms we accept the self-understanding that each co-op has and we do not prejudge their form of co-operation. This subjective viewpoint is an essential factor in any classification of co-operatives.

Second, these political terms are used by those outside the co-ops to describe co-ops in their society. They are terms used by sociologists, economists, political scientists, and other experts in explaining the nature of these organizations. For example, an American farmer-owned purchasing co-op is generally considered by American historians as a populist reaction to the domination of industrialists, and Hutterite communities are described by sociologists as successful examples of communalism.

Third, these four designations reflect the tendency of co-operative in-stitutions "to take their characteristics and features from the general en-vironment in which they exist."[31] A country's legal statutes on property and social relations are the product of the political ideology that is domi-nant in that society. It is these statutes that circumscribe co-operative practice.[32] The four ideologies that are used here represent the basic categories that operate in today's world. They describe in a general way different political environments.

Fourth, this typology is able to account for every major co-operative and collective form developed in the last 150 years. It does so without creating a mass of different categories between which only small dif-ferences exist. It takes into account the major ideological developments of this century and allows us to see the similarities and differences bet-ween a worker co-op in Spain and a credit union in Winnipeg.

Finally, the choice of political terms is an acknowledgement of the primacy of political ideology in shaping socio-economic relations. But it does not mean that co-ops must only be understood in political terms. They can and must be viewed in other ways as well. The reason I have chosen the dimension of political ideology is that it often encompasses other viewpoints. In it are expressed religious, sociological, philosophical, and economic perspectives, which are whole in themselves but are also part of a general social system whose essence is compressed and dis-tilled by ideology.

The first tradition that will be considered is the liberal democratic one. This term refers to all those co-operatives that are formally incorporated in societies in which capitalism and the marketplace predominate. This is the case in Western Europe and North America. The words liberal democratic refer to those co-operative businesses which have the characteristics of capitalist organizations, while viewing themselves as noncapitalist and populist.[33] In Europe, where left-wing politics is more common, 'social democratic' is another possible term. Social democracy is a political philosophy that accepts capitalism as the dominant form, while seeking to redistribute wealth more equitably. European co-operators are more comfortable seeing themselves linked to socialism, while North American co-operators are not. Since this book will be focus-ing on Canada as an example of the Rochdale model, it would be more appropriate to use the term 'liberal democratic.'

Co-operatives in capitalist countries reflect an essential duality. On the one hand they support the marketplace, while on the other they work hard to make sure that their kind of organization, rather than the capitalist kind that created the market, makes inroads. The social democratic ideology of liberal democratic co-ops is evident in the fact that Britain's

Co-operative Party eventually united with the Labour Party, Britain's social democratic party.[34] In Western Canada, the Rochdale co-ops prefer to be viewed as politically neutral. But one thing is clear—co-operatives in this tradition have a very high respect for the private property of their members.[35]

The second tradition is the Marxist one. It encompasses those co-operative and collective forms developed by Marxist-Leninist societies in which the market has only a minor role and state domination of the means of production and distribution is the norm. In communist societies, private property exists and is tolerated but is generally severely limited. In the communist tradition we will be examining the kolkhoz of the Soviet Union, the commune in China, and workers self-management in Yugo-slavia. Just as there is variety in liberal democratic co-ops, so there is varie-ty in Marxist ones. The kolkhoz is different from the commune and the commune is different from a Yugoslavian firm. But in every case the em-phasis is on the development of society as a whole rather than on in-dividual interests. What is most crucial about communist co-operative firms is that they are integrated into centrally-planned and managed economies that are state-dominated. Those co-ops which are not unique creations of Marxist-Leninist ideology but are liberal democratic in origin and yet operate in communist systems, such as farmer co-ops in Poland, will not be discussed here.

The third tradition is the socialist one. One author has described this tradition in the following way:

> For socialists, the objective of co-operation is not the increase in the assets of individuals, but the taking of another step to socialism by lessening the importance of private property.[36]

The socialist category refers to those co-operative and collective forms that have been created by socialist ideologies which are not Marxist-Leninist. These co-ops are more radical than liberal democratic ones because they are usually multi-functional in nature. They provide a vari-ety of co-operative activities for their members rather than the liberal democratic model of one function per co-op. Socialist co-operatives have a more negative view of private property than liberal democratic ones and are more community-oriented in structure. Unlike Marxist co-operatives they maintain a distance from the state and participate in a market economy in most cases. In this tradition are the kibbutzim of Israel, the ujamaa villages of Tanzania, and the worker co-ops of Mondragon in the Basque region of Spain. Socialist co-ops tend to emphasize co-operation in both production and consumption, while liberal democratic ones are either one or the other. Also, nationalist factors have moulded

11

socialist co-ops into indigenous forms that are not found elsewhere.

The fourth tradition is the communalist one. Communalist ideology is the ideology of intentional communities with a very high degree of member commitment in which collective production and consumption are fundamental.[37] Communalism emphasizes egalitarianism and collective ownership with a severe restriction on private property. Unlike the collective forms set up by the state in communist societies, the communes of this tradition are usually found in capitalist countries but far outside the mainstream of the society in which they exist. They are usually short-lived and economically marginal.[38] Laurence Veysey, who studied the phenomenon closely, describes the communalist tradition as one based on small groups of people who "set themselves apart from the everyday society of their time and place, hoping to create more intense and closely knit communities."[39]

The section on the communalist tradition is divided into two parts. The first deals with the religious communes and includes both Catholic monasticism and Protestant utopian communities. In Western Canada, the religious aspect is represented by the Hutterites, the Doukhobours, and monasteries. The second part is the secular tradition that includes early nineteenth century utopian communities such as those established by Robert Owen in both England and the United States, and twentieth century counterculture communes of the late Sixties and early Seventies. This political tradition is represented in Western Canada by the Matador farm co-op in Saskatchewan.

Henri Desroche has stated that the history of co-operatives can be plotted on a graph whose vertical dimension is the unifunctional co-operative and whose horizontal dimension is the multifunctional co-op community.[40] Historically, the vertical dimension has been dominant and more successful because of its wide appeal with a minimum of involvement, but the horizontal dimension persists and every so often increases in popularity. The liberal democratic tradition is definitely of the vertical dimension. So is the communist tradition because of its state integration. The socialist and communalist traditions are closer to the horizontal dimension. They are often sporadic and isolated phenomena when considered on a global scale, but both socialist and communalist forms contain examples of long-term success.

The four traditions outline the basic modes in which co-operation has expressed itself. Although not every national co-operative and collective form is discussed in this book, it is fair to say that the sampling provided is sufficient to give the reader an insight into the essential characteristics of each tradition. These characteristics will then be related to the new social co-operative form discussed in part two of the book.

THE SEARCH FOR COMMUNITY

Chapter Two:
THE LIBERAL DEMOCRATIC TRADITION

A DEFINITION

The three basic characteristics that distinguish liberal democratic co-ops from other co-operative ventures are first, an emphasis on private property; second, a basic tolerance of capitalism; third, a pragmatic unifunctionalism. These characteristics evolved out of the Rochdale model during the nineteenth century and have come to define most of the co-operative institutions prevalent in Western Europe and North America.

The Rochdale principles made no direct statement one way or the other about private property as such. Yet in aggregate they resulted in an affirmation of private property while promoting co-operative ownership. If at first this seems like a contradiction, it is not when one realizes what is involved in co-op ownership under the Rochdale rules. The practice of one person/one vote is a democratic assault on the capitalist practice of tying the power of ownerhsip to the number of shares one held. Likewise the principle of limited return on capital is meant to remove the profit motive from co-ops so that they will not become tools of speculation. But co-operators are not restricted to investing solely in co-operative institutions. They have a right to enjoy and dispose of their income as they see fit. The dividend on patronage is a confirmation of a nonegalitarian approach.

When a person joins a credit union he deposits funds as his or her private property to be withdrawn on demand. Likewise a farmer who belongs to a co-operative wheat pool markets his privately produced grain through the organization and is reimbursed on an individual basis in direct proportion to the produce he has sold through the co-op. Membership in the co-op does not restrict or impinge upon his private ownership of his assets or its products other than his voluntary agreement to market his produce through it.

The Rochdale rules created a consumer movement "resting on a solid foundation of retail trade."[1] The concept of patronage based on purchase of goods left the issue of private property intact. The area where co-operative ownership could have affected private ownership most was in industry, but this sector remained the least co-operatized. What came out of the Rochdale model of co-operation was an emphasis on individual return and individual benefit. In 1914 the anarchist theorist Kropotkin used the term "co-operative egotism" to describe Western European co-operatives.[2] He felt that these co-ops were meant to protect private property and not encourage sharing. Recently, a British scholar wrote that "most co-operators would agree that the aim is to enable the survival of the small units of production and consumption."[3] Although this was not the goal of the Rochdale pioneers, it was a result of the liberal democratic movement that operated in capitalist society.

The consumer orientation of the liberal democratic model helped private ownership by not reaching into other fundamental areas of human life. It was not co-operation but competition that influenced people's mentality. G.D.H. Cole was refering to British consumer co-ops when he wrote in 1951: "Co-operators...often object to any form of employee representation on the ground that it is the consumer's money that is at stake."[4] This viewpoint works on behalf of the individual accumulation of wealth and divides producers from consumers.

Liberal democratic co-operatives not only emphasize private property but also tolerate the capitalist system as a whole. Because co-operatives developed "at a time when there was very little state or public enterprise as we know it today," they were viewed as, and acted as, alternatives to privately-owned business.[5] But they never replaced capitalism in any real sense. Instead they adapted to the dominant principles of free enterprise, whose main feature next to private property is the marketplace. These co-ops were created within the capitalist system to lower prices for consumers, to increase prices to producers, to control supply and to negotiate collective demands. So their structures were tuned to operate in the marketplace. The early co-op idealists believed, because co-ops were so popular, that they would eventually displace capitalist enterprise, but their gradualist approach meant they had to play by the rules of the capitalist system.

The rules of the marketplace have their own dynamic in which co-operatives were quickly enmeshed. As capitalist production evolved into ever larger and more monopolistic practices, co-operatives had to follow suit in order to compete. The systems stage of co-operation is a direct result of that marketplace competitiveness. The modes of operation and labour relations developed by capitalist firms became part of co-operative reality as well.

Co-operative tolerance of capitalism was a necessity that turned into a virtue. It was their pragmatism that made Rochdale-style co-ops popular and successful. They did well in the marketplace and so they had no reason to fight for its elimination. Their members joined co-ops not to end capitalism but to improve their personal economic situation. Liberal democratic co-ops were integrated into the dominant system right from the start.

The essence of liberal democratic co-ops is successful competition with capitalism through short-term and immediate benefits to its members. This pragmatic approach appealed to the person's self-interest rather than to his idealism and it demanded a reconciliation between the co-operative and the private sectors.

Liberal democratic co-ops parallel the trade union experience in Western Europe and North America. Unions represented those who benefited least from the economic system and challenged capitalism the way co-ops did. They asserted worker rights, negotiated improved conditions, and became an important feature of society. But they never sought the end of capitalism, only the improvement of their members share of the economic system. Trade unions, like co-ops, had to adopt this stance because they found it was the surest and easiest way to advancement. Partial answers and small immediate victories gave their members something tangible, which in turn reinforced this approach. Very quickly this became the norm.

The third characteristic of liberal democratic co-ops is their unifunctionalism. They operate best when they focus on a single economic issue rather than dealing with the whole system. Henrik Infield, a prominent sociologist of co-operation, described the situation well when he wrote:

> The vast majority of co-operative associations still remain of the segmented type. Membership in a consumer store, a credit union, a marketing or purchasing co-operative affects the individual only in one of his many social roles, that of a buyer of groceries, borrower of money, trader of agricultural products or implements. The changes required in this case extend merely to one segment of the individual's social behaviour and can be carried through with a minimum of effort. It also remains...extremely limited in its effect on the behaviour of the individual as a whole.[6]

This compartmentalization of co-operation resulted from dealing with specific, single areas of operation. By restricting co-operation to one area, co-ops allowed nonco-operative influences to dominate the actions of their members. For members of liberal democratic co-ops involvement consists of partial, highly restricted commitments none of which is profound. The results of this approach are evident in the following statistical information. A 1956 study of British consumer co-operatives in their mature phase showed a member participation rate of a mere 0.5 to 1.65 percent. This contrasted with British agricultural producer co-ops that had a participation rate of 10 to 15 percent.[7] Minimal involvement has resulted in Western European and North American co-ops being described as "the least socialised [co-operative] organization."[8]

But this minimum involvement, resulting from a pragmatic, unifunctional approach, is precisely what makes them attractive and effective in capitalist societies. Over one hundred million people belong to one kind of co-operative or another in Western Europe and North America, yet this vast membership does not threaten the dominant capitalist mode of production. Based on a strict voluntarism, liberal democratic co-ops have evolved into finely tuned examples of coexistence. They demand little from their members while offering them favourable terms of participation in the economy.

Because these co-ops compete with private business on terms and conditions determined by the private sector, their sense of reform is rather limited. They have discovered a niche in the system and like other institutions work diligently to protect it. In the systems phase the dream of replacing the private sector has disappeared and has been replaced with the theory of co-ops as a 'third sector' in a capitalist economy behind the private and public sectors.

THE INTERNATIONAL CO-OPERATIVE ALLIANCE

The International Co-operative Alliance, founded in 1895, has proved to be an organization in which conflict and division are as common as co-operation. Up to World War I, the ICA remained overwhelmingly made up of Consumer Societies."[9] The consumer societies viewed other co-ops "with suspicion."[10] Since the main feature of liberal democratic co-ops is individual return, it was inevitable that consumer co-ops would clash with producer co-ops. The ICA has seen its share of such battles but they pale before the ideological battles between various co-operative traditions.[11]

After World War I the main issues in the ICA was the status of co-operatives in the new Soviet state. Since political neutrality and voluntary membership were part of the original rules, the communist emphasis on state control was perceived as a serious difficulty. (Interestingly the political neutrality rule had already been broken by the British with their own Co-operative Party.) The debate was resolved when the New Economic Policy was adopted in the Twenties. Autonomy returned to Soviet co-ops. Then under Stalin the urban consumer co-op network was integrated into the state bureaucracy and ceased to belong to the ICA. But a new debate then developed over the status of the co-operative farm called the kolkhoz. In 1937 the ICA adopted four of the original eight Rochdale principles as basic to the definition of co-operation. Although voluntary membership was one of these, it was never enforced and was simply interpreted as meaning open membership with democratic control. Although the kolkhoz was not voluntary it was accepted as a legitimate co-op. No wonder Valko once wrote that "there is no general theory which can be pronounced as an exclusive and consistent philosophy of co-operation."[12] In the Sixties the ICA increased to six the number of applicable rules.

Laidlaw described co-ops as occupying "the middle ground between...the public sector and...the private."[13] They are the middle ground because they adopt features from both and they gravitate toward the sector that is most prominent in their society. They are also in the middle because they represent neither the private firm nor the politically controlled public firm. In a country like Sweden consumer co-ops are dominant in retail trade. In the Soviet Union the state-created collective farm has only marginal autonomy next to its cousin, the state farm. The American agricultural co-operatives encourage private production and "the economic structure of co-operation" compared to the collective life of the kolkhoz.[14] In order to maintain its claim to global representation, the ICA represents all kinds of co-operatives, both American and Russian.

The Canadian experience is primarily of the liberal democratic kind. Canadian co-operative federations are part of the ICA and represent Western European and British-inspired co-operative practices. As part of the international capitalist economy, Canada has tended to limit co-operative experience to the strict Rochdale model. Because of this, the Canadian experience is a good example of the liberal democratic form.

CANADIAN CO-OPERATION

A recent federal government study showed that 43 percent of adult Canadians belonged to at least one co-operative and co-op membership stood at 12.6 million in 1981.[15] This puts Canada into the top range of countries with co-operatives.[16] The co-op sector in Canada owned or controlled more than $45 billion in assets. But its revenue represented less than 5 percent of the total for all Canadian business.[17] Co-operatives are so popular in Canada that in Quebec over four million people belong to credit unions and in Saskatchewan over half the population belongs to both financial and nonfinancial co-ops. In spite of this co-ops lack any substantial clout in the national economy as a whole.

Historically, co-operative institutions have developed in Canada on a regional basis. They have done so because of the cultural differences in a bilingual country, because of the different regional economies that have developed in Canada, and because of the varying historical periods during which the country was settled and developed. A recent study described Canadian co-ops as "emerging out of local initiatives, immigration patterns, and group interests."[18] What that study showed was that co-ops developed as subordinate manifestations of some other economic or social program: that is, these social and economic programs or movements turned to co-ops as vehicles to achieve goals other than purely co-operative ones. In Atlantic Canada, there was an adult education movement, the Antigonish Movement, which fostered co-ops. In Quebec credit unions called 'caisses populaires', were expressions of francophone nationalism. And in Western Canada the wheat pools were the economic vehicles for regional discontent at central Canadian domination.

Each region of the country developed a specific area of co-operation in which it excelled. This regionalism produced a healthy diversity of co-operative institutions, but it also meant that the movement itself was divided regionally and did not develop a single, unified national image or identity. It was only a few years ago that co-ops could even seek incorporation under a general federal co-operative act.

The Antigonish Movement was developed in Nova Scotia during the 1920s and 1930s by two university priests—J.J. Tompkins and Moses Coady. Through small group discussion they were able to mobilize large segments of the population to launch economic organizations for community improvement. By 1934, 952 study clubs had been formed in Nova Scotia and 150 co-operative enterprises had been set up.[19] The movement touched fishermen, farmers, and miners through credit unions, co-operative canneries, and marketing co-ops. During the Depression the Antigonish Movement became an important regional vehicle of survival for ordinary people.

Quebec's contribution to Canada's co-operative mosaic was the credit union as we know it. The first 'caisse populaire' was established by a legislative reporter named Alphonse Desjardins. Working in his own community of Levis, he launched a movement that has now grown to such a size that in Quebec there are more credit unions than branches of chartered banks and trust companies.[20] The powerful Catholic Church promoted credit unions in every parish as expressions of Quebecois loyalty and piety. The caisses populaires now play a crucial role in the Quebec government's economic planning and have been called by one contemporary observer, "un systeme economique hypersophistique."[21]

Ideologically, Canadian co-operatives followed the general trend of liberal democratic co-ops by offering "a powerful emphasis on self-interested pragmatism."[22] Out of that pragmatism came the world's one-time largest credit union (Vancouver City Savings Credit Union) with 130,000 members and $1.3 billion in assets.[23] It also created Canada's largest property and casualty insurance company—the Co-operators.[24] Canadian co-operation has also followed the utopian-movement-systems phase of the liberal democratic tradition. By examining the Western Canadian component of Canadian co-operation we can view this evolution in detail.

WESTERN CANADIAN CO-OPERATION: THE PRAIRIE EXPERIENCE

The Western Canadian co-operative movement developed along with the transformation of the West from a fur trade into a wheat economy. Between 1901 and 1911 more than one million immigrants came to the Prairies to create the region's farms, villages, and cities.[25] These pioneers came from Europe, the United States, and central Canada to create one of the world's leading grain-based economies. They built an agrarian way of life with its own economic and political institutions, which dominated the region for fifty years.

Co-operative ideas first came to the Prairies in the 1870s with American farmers who migrated north. They brought with them such populist organizations as the Grange, which in turn was replaced by an even more militant American farm organization called the Patrons of Industry. However these organizations never took hold permanently because agriculture was still developing in the region and the American parent organizations were themselves beset by probems and failures. It was not until the turn of the century that local co-operative institutions began to develop.

It was the "long history of exploitation by profit-motivated institutions with head offices located outside the region" that pushed co-ops to the forefront.[26] At their 1982 convention in Brandon, Manitoba the Patrons of Industry called for farmer-owned grain elevators and flour mills, but it was not until a decade later that there was significant development in this area. Pioneering farmers who had suffered the great hardship of homesteading were angered by the monopoly held by grain elevator companies, by their high storage charges, unfair dockage, and tampered

21

weight scales.[27] Likewise the speculative practices of the grain traders on the Grain Exchange in Winnipeg meant a poor return for the farmer. And when the farmer had sold his wheat, he then had to face a National Policy which favoured central Canadian manufacturers. Protected by tariffs, they were able to charge the farmer high prices, while he had to sell his products in the marketplace without any protection. The farmer was trapped by a low and unstable income at one end and high prices at the other.

In his classic study of the wheat economy, the historian V.C.Fowke summarized the situation of the farmer in the following way:

> The farmers in the prairie provinces protested repeatedly, if not continuously, against their position in the price system throughout the decades which marked the establishment and development of the Canadian wheat economy...They proposed far-reaching reforms...state ownership...removal of the tariff wall...In particular cases they sought to combat monopoly by co-operative organization and production.[28]

Their breakthrough came with the formation of the Grain Growers Grain Company in 1905. (It was later renamed United Grain Growers.) Founded by E.A. Partridge, the father of Western Canada's producer co-operatives, and his fellow farmers of Sintaluta, Saskatchewan, the GGGC became one of the cornerstones of the co-operative movement in Western Canada. Owned by farmers on a one person/one vote basis, the Company quickly challenged the private grain traders. It secured a seat on the Grain Exchange and began to sell wheat. In spite of determined opposition from private companies, the GGGC prevailed and established itself as the first large-scale and long-term producer co-op in the West.

Farm co-ops were an integral part of what has come to be known as the 'agrarian revolt.'[29] At the turn of the century, 75 percent of the Prairie population was rural and it remained at 60 to 65 percent right up to World War II.[30] This meant the farm consitituency had electoral muscle. In 1909 farmers organized the United Farmers of Alberta, which eventually went into politics and became the government of the province from 1921 to 1935. Under the UFA umbrella co-operatives sprang up all over the province. The Alberta Farmers Co-operative Elevator Company was formed in 1913 and amalgamated with the Grain Growers in 1917. Saskatchewan had developed an equivalent in 1911. In 1915 the three grain marketing organizations had 60,000 members. They owned 400 elevators, handled 80 million bushels of wheat, and distributed 4,000 carloads of supplies.[31]

The twenty year period from 1900 to 1920 can be considered the 'utopian' phase of Prairie co-operation. There were impressive developments in marketing and purchasing but the mechanism of elevator companies, a seat on the Grain Exchange, and bulk buying was still incomplete. Farmers were not yet able to influence basic grain prices because they had little power to control the supply and demand mechanism of the marketplace. In 1923 an American named Aaron Sapiro came to Saskatchewan to promote the idea of a wheat pool. He had already successfully established pools among American tobacco and citrus fruit growers. The idea was simple enough. It required that farmers sign agreements to market their produce for a fixed period through a central organization. This allowed farmers to regulate the flow of grain to market and so influence prices.

The pool idea so galvanized prairie farmers that within a year each of the prairie provinces had a wheat pool and had signed up over half the wheat acreage in the region. The pools represented the 'movement' phase of co-operation. In the period form 1920 to 1945 they brought the farm producer co-ops to their highest level. The pools remain a powerful force in prairie agriculture today. The Saskatchewan Wheat Pool had assets of one billion dollars in 1983 and it ranked 37th in sales among Canadian companies.[32] Altogether the four Western grain co-ops now handle about 80 percent of Western grain.[33]

It was the Depression of the Thirties that consolidated the co-operative movement's special relationship with the region. The terrible hardships faced by farmers encouraged all sorts of new ventures including the world's first co-operative refinery in Regina, a spate of credit unions promoted by Moses Coady of the Antigonish Movement and George Keen, General-Secretary of the Co-operative Union of Canada. Co-ops organized educational and social programs in every part of the region. It was during this time that the co-operative philosophy of democratizing the economic system and defending the livelihood of ordinary people found its widest appeal. This spirit is evident in the following statement which appeared in the tenth Annual Report of the Saskatchewan Co-operative Wheat Producers Limited:

> The co-operative movement is, in fact, the outstanding example in the world of planned economic effort, and the whole hope of civilization lies in its extension, not only co-operation within the nation, but co-operation among the nations. Unrestrained competition, the jungle law of strife and struggle in the economic sphere, will only intensify the distress born of poverty; international co-operation will bring the peace and security which are not only

necessary for present recovery, but are fundamental to the persistence of civilization.[34]

After World War II this spirit receded and the farm co-ops had entered into their 'systems' phase, which accelerated after 1960. In this phase the farm co-ops generated their own web of institutions. They formed second and third tier co-ops in which there were no individual members, only other co-ops or co-op federations. These included the wholesale societies such as Federated Co-op, Co-op Trust, Canadian Co-operative Implements Ltd. and the Co-operative Insurance Company. Instead of the great mass movements that propelled co-operative growth, there were corporate structures expanding and augmenting the power of the system.

The impulse for social reform quietly dissipated and then disappeared. This loss of popular energy resulted from broad social changes in society. In 1946 25 percent of the Canadian labor force was in agriculture. By 1981 it was only 3 percent.[35] In 1941 over half the people of the region were rural but by 1971 that had dropped to 16 percent.[36] At the same time, the capital value of farms increased from $6,565 to $72,805.[37] There were fewer farmers and larger farms. Between 1971 and 1981, the number of family farms in Western Canada declined from 180,000 to 120,000.[38]

Population shifts to the city meant that the economic focus of the region, especially in the 1970s, was on nonagricultural resources such as oil and gas. But co-operative institutions remained tied to their rural roots. They manufactured and distributed fertilizer, processed food, and in general served their traditional membership. In 1983 the four western producer co-ops had sales of $5.4 billion.[39] They were powerful, wealthy, and yet limited in their scope.

Credit unions grew in popularity during the 'systems' phase. People continued to join in ever-increasing numbers, yet the number of credit unions continued to decrease as corporate rationalization was implemented. The number of credit unions peaked in 1965 and since then the total has decreased by one-third.[40] Wherever there was a popular pressure for new areas of co-operation, the traditional co-op institutions were usually far behind. During the 1970s a new co-op housing sector based on government social housing policy developed on its own as did the so-called 'emerging' co-ops which established health food co-ops and day care centres. The co-op system did learn its lesson and is now actively involved in developing worker co-ops in Canada.

In the movement phase, it was mass participation that governed the speed and scope of co-operative development. In the systems phase participation is no longer crucial because the system is centralized and self-perpetuating. A typical contemporary co-operative experience is that of the person who is a client or customer of the Co-operators and whose relationship to it is purely that of a consumer. He has no rights of membership. In the past twenty-five years this has become the new norm. The result is a degradation of co-operative ideals as well as a conservatism which refuses to develop any significant areas of co-operation that were not underway already decades ago.[41] It is quantitative expansion that takes precedence over qualitative development. In his 1968 research paper, T.D. Harris of the University of Manitoba wrote:

> Recent features of co-operative development [in the West] may be summarized as having consisted of a) physical consolidation of certain commercial operations, b) increased centralization of formal organizational structures, and c) attempts at evolving for co-operation an integrative development and expansion system.[42]

This is to be expected in terms of the three-phase model. In the systems phase, there is no idealistic, utopian energy to generate new beginnings. Alexander Laidlaw wrote bluntly about the change from movement to systems phase:

> The biggest change I've seen in my lifetime...is the shift of power and decision-making from the local to the central or secondary organization...now locals are generally compelled to operate within the framework of central policy or suffer the consequences.[43]

In the sophisticated and rapidly changing urban environment where today's consumer co-ops need to exist, there is a lack of community roots and identity. The co-op means discount prices. The result is a method of operation which is alienated from popular input:

> For example, FCL and B.C. Central Credit Union established a joint committee in 1978 to promote the development of co-op stores in B.C. where their market penetration was low...Obviously the necessary share capital does not come primarily from new members, but from FCL and BCCCU.[44]

When co-operation becomes a way of business rather than a way of life the missionary zeal of the earlier period becomes an embarrassment. It upsets corporate strategy and threatens corporate interests. As one government official put it recently, "They don't have anyone working in the street. They all work in offices." Grant Mitchell, former deputy minister of Saskatchewan's Department of Co-operation and Co-operative Development and also former president of Saskatchewan's largest credit union (Sherwood), pointed out that the economies of scale needed by the co-op system have yet to be matched by a democratically controlled system.[45]

The co-operative system in Western Canada has reached its present stage of development over an eighty-year period. The utopian phase saw significant initiatives on the part of farmers, which were superseded in the movement phase with the fundamental co-operative institutions that presently exists. After World War II the declining importance of agriculture and the dramatic decrease in rural population forced the co-ops into a systems phase in which they consolidated their traditional services. Like all liberal democratic co-ops, those of Western Canada sought to develop a pragmatic relationship with capitalism. Co-operation as a "harbinger of a new society" was not a realistic possibility.[46] Mutual aid and co-operation as a way of life, which still made sense in the movement phase, evaporated with the new, large farms and the business approach to production. The movement phase resulted from the existence of a relatively unified agrarian bloc, while in the systems phase farmers became a small, relatively heterogeneous group.[47]

Co-operative development on the prairies paralleled political movements. In the utopian phase there was a strong anti-traditional party sentiment and the desire to develop an indigenous politics. Formations like the Non-Partisan League and the United Farmers of Alberta, with its philosophy of "group government," were typical. The national manifestation of this thinking was the Progressive movement which rose and fell in the 1920s. Third-party politics were the hallmark of agrarian protest during the Depression with the founding of both the Social Credit Party and the Co-operative Commonwealth Federation. In its manifesto, the CCF called for "the establishment in Canada of a Co-operative Commonwealth in which the principle regulating production, distribution, and exchange will be the supply of human needs and not the making of profits." This was an acknowledgement of the strength of co-operation during the movement phase. So it was not surprising that Canada's first social democratic government was elected in Saskatchewan in 1944, in the province where co-operatives were predominant.

In the interwar years, there were two distinct strains in prairie co-operation. The first was represented by Henry Wise Wood, president of the United Farmers of Alberta from 1916 to 1931 and president of the Alberta Wheat Pool from 1923 to 1937. Wood emphasized economic organization as the key to agrarian power and was opposed to political involvement. The second strain was represented by J.S. Woodsworth, the first national leader of the CCF. As a member of parliament for more than two decades the emphasized political organization and encouraged farm-labour links, which Wood was not keen on.[48] The movement was broad enough to contain both elements.

In the postwar period, a new prairie society emerged that differed from its rural, agrarian past. The movements of social reform and their political and economic manifestations entered a time of consolidation and entrenchment. The wheat economy was no longer king and the driving force of economic change were crown corporations and multinational energy companies.[49] With their newly diminished role, co-operative institutions began to re-examine their identity. Because they were losing their position of economic and political leadership, the agrarian co-ops wanted to re-evaluate their future. The Co-operative Future Directions Project which they funded in the late Seventies and early Eighties was a major reassessment of their condition. It will be discussed more fully later in the book. At this point what is important is that the system did engage in self-examination.

We can get a good grasp of the nature of Western Canadian co-ops by seeing how they reflect the three basic characteristics of liberal democratic co-ops: respect for private property, tolerance of capitalism, and unifunctionalism. Throughout their evolution the agrarian co-ops viewed themselves as protectors of individual farm property. They opposed any form of communalization or socialization of the family farm. The marketing mechanisms they created were there to influence the marketplace, not to eliminate it. Pragmatism meant co-operating in developing one's own personal wealth. This basic economic orientation had a superstructure of cultural and social life in the movement phase which was appropriate to a rural economy before large-scale mechanization. When technology changed farming, these social aspects went the way of the horse. The co-ops were unifunctional in their goals and this encouraged minimalist involvement. That great wheat pools based on producers still had some vital member participation but the consumer co-op movement in the growing cities was the epitome of non-involvement.

Co-ops in Western Canada are strict adherents of the Rochdale model. They have always represented the Anglo-American tradition in co-operation. But they do have features that are distinctly their own. First, it was an agrarian society and its farm producers that gave vitality to Western Canadian co-operation. Co-operation was not dominated by consumer co-ops the way it was in England. Second, co-operative institutions were part of a general regional economic protest that created indigenous political parties and social movements that oppposed central Canadian domination. The co-ops were expressions of a sectional desire for control over its destiny. Third, Western Canadian co-ops were not peripheral nor minor factors in the region's economy. They represented the wishes of the majority. These farm producer origins, the links to regionalism, and the general importance of the co-ops in the West's economy and political history are the legacy of the movement in Western Canada. How that legacy will affect future development will be discussed in the second part of this book.

THE IDEOLOGY OF LIBERAL DEMOCRATIC CO-OPS

Although the meaning of the term 'ideology' is often debated and has proven difficult to define, it is generally considered to refer to a set of ideas which explain or promote certain ways of acting in society.[50] Sometimes it refers to any belief system, while at other times it is strictly limited to political ideas. Karl Marx introduced the concept into modern social thought by using the term to denote the dominant ideas of the ruling class. Since he considered their use of ideology to be that of a misleading justification of an exploitative system, ideology came to connote false consciousness.

This negative use has been continued by North American anti-Marxists, who use the term ideology to refer to Marx's ideas or any that seek the overthrow of capitalism. Both Marxists and anti-Marxists use it as a derogatory term. I prefer to use it in a less polemical manner. In this book, ideology refers to that set of ideas which is generated by a group to defend its self-interests. It is a doctrine that justifies certain economic and political ways of acting. It moulds thinking on social and political relations and, like all justifications, it contradicts itself when it does not achieve its stated ideals. Ideologies are an intellectual defense of or an intellectual attack on class and group interests and they are found in every society. In fact, societies cannot operate without ideologies to rationalize conduct.

Modern European co-ops arose out of the failure of utopian socialist communities of the first half of the nineteenth century to transform society. Since these communities were unable to provide a successful anwer to the vast social problems created by capitalist industrialization, the Rochdale model rid itself of this community focus and turned to the service of individual, specific economic interests. The ethics of individual improvement and advancement through hard work, labour discipline and thrift, moral elevation, abstinence and the cultivation of personal virtues and personal salvation was the starting-point of nineteenth century consumer co-ops.[51] But as culture and history evolved this puritanical perspective fell by the wayside and consumerism as such became the main perspective. What Rochdale co-ops encouraged was a gradual amelioration of each individual's situation through participation in co-ops, and like the earlier utopian phase they did not bring and end to the dominant system.

The Rochdale ideology was primarily one of liberal democracy. The concept of one person/one vote was a famous nineteenth century cry for reform by the vast disenfranchised majority. It was a working class demand. Likewise the limited return on capital was suited to workers who had no capital and needed a system of saving to meet the demands of a minimal standard of living. Workers needed to borrow money for essentials and not for speculation. They needed to save on the cost of basics like food and shelter and were not concerned about what dividends they drew. Just as political democracy maintained the social *status quo*, so co-ops provided an economic democracy that maintained the capitalist system.

For workers and farmers to own economic institutions was part of this democratization. But the fundamental voluntariness of participation meant that co-ops could succeed only when they were good competitors in the general system. Loyalty to the co-op was maintained by material benefits; if these disappeared, the co-op disappeared. There was little else to keep one attached to it. Although co-ops saw themselves as an 'alternative' to capitalism they had to match their capitalist competitors in serving their customers. This rationale eventually caused them to downplay co-op ideology and ideals. The seeds of this were already sown in the rejection of utopian communities.

Like the trade union movement that evolved simultaneously with liberal democratic co-ops, the emphasis was on immediate economic demands and the gradual amelioration of conditions through negotiation with capitalism. There was a fundamental commitment to peaceful change which would not threaten the class structure and economic system of society.

Western Canadian co-ops fit into this general approach. They had a strong commitment to the common man and they offered practical solutions to his immediate needs, but always within the limits of the liberal democratic society and its commitment to private property and the marketplace. These co-ops had nothing to do with utopian schemes. They were democratic but not egalitarian. They were vehicles for certain groups to compete. They helped the dispossessed and the alienated to get a little more. They provided a refuge within the system.

Liberal democratic co-ops carry within their ideology several basic contradictions. These contradictions have influenced the historical evolution of the Rochdale co-ops. First there is the contradiction between utopian and pragmatic goals. In the initial stage of liberal democratic co-ops in England and Canada there was considerable analysis of the state of society and its ills.[52] There was hope for the development of a co-operative commonwealth to replace capitalism and co-operators felt that piecemeal, pragmatic organizations would do it. Their pragmatism made them popular but that popularity was never converted into control because co-ops were not geared to converting a whole system. They had been set up primarily to challenge specific aspects of the economic process and not bring in a new society. After 150 years, these co-ops remain a distant third sector. If anything it has been the public sector that has grown to challenge the private sector. During this period the world has seen major revolutionary changes in various political economies, which have resulted in totally different kinds of co-operative structures coming into existence.

Second, there is the contradiction between the promotion of individual self-interest and the promotion of co-operation. While praising co-operation among people as an ideal, these co-ops have promoted individual self-interest. They have adopted the capitalist competitive ethic in order to survive in the marketplace and they have shown their members how co-operation can make them better off than their neighbour.

Third, there is a contradiction between their emphasis on popular participation and control and their emphasis on sound management and corporate growth. The proliferation of second and third tier co-ops has been necessitated by the demands of the marketplace but this has meant decreasing popular input and democratic control in favour of more formalized structures, which require a managerial class for their operation.

Fourth, there is a contradiction between producer and consumer co-ops. Originally, co-operation among consumers and co-operation among producers was to be resolved through equal membership in a co-operative community. This dream disappeared quickly. As co-ops became individual units, competition became as common as co-operation. The kind of loyalty which liberal democratic co-ops fostered was that of the self-centred individual.

Liberal democratic co-ops are ideologically closer to capitalism than to co-operative institutions in noncapitalist countries. Although they continue to describe themselves as an alternative, most members' experience of them parallels those they have with nonco-operative institutions. One wheat pool representative has been quoted as saying that young farmers in Western Canada see nothing that distinguishes the pool from Cargill or other large corporations.[53]

The following examination of co-ops in noncapitalist countries will show what a profound contrast exists between the liberal democratic co-ops of the Rochdale model and their communist counterparts.

Chapter Three:
THE MARXIST TRADITION

A DEFINITION

The Marxist tradition is a twentieth century phenomenon whose co-operative forms of organization are only fifty years old compared to the 140 year old liberal democratic tradition. In spite of this youth, the Marxist tradition provides the political and economic framework for the lives of 1.5 billion people, many of whom participate in co-operative organizations, which are the antithesis of co-ops in capitalist societies.

Karl Marx was a nineteenth century European thinker whose ideas have become the basis for this century's most successful revolutionary movements. The Rochdale model was the dominant form of co-op in Marx's lifetime (1818-1883). He viewed liberal democatic co-ops as providing some benefit to the workers, but he did not view them as crucial to the creation of a worker-controlled society.

In his writings Marx attacked the capitalist system and explained how it would be replaced by a communist society. The first of these societies came into existence in Russia thirty-five years after his death. Its approach to co-operatives reflected both a general Marxist ideology and specific elements. The same happened in other countries which adopted communist principles. Because Marx was critical of liberal democratic co-ops and because he envisaged wholly new forms of economic and social organization in a society without capitalism, it was to be expected that societies calling themselves Marxist would create their own original forms of co-operative enterprise.

Marx was a socialist who claimed that other socialist thinkers were utopian. These thinkers (Fourier, Proudhon, St. Simon and Owen) were the very ones who had promoted various forms of failed or unrealized co-operative communities.[1] While the Rochdale model with its vision of a voluntary, gradual replacement of capitalist relations was one practical answer to the utopians, Marx taught a completely different solution. He called his thinking 'scientific socialism' to distinguish it from the 'utopian' kind. He claimed to have discovered the scientific laws that propelled capitalist economies and would eventually bring about their downfall. Marx viewed history as a history of classes that rose to prominence with a particular kind of economy and then were overthrown by a rising new class. Just as the bourgeoisie had overthrown feudalism, so would workers overthrow capitalism and create a communist society. In a communist society, the workers would own the means of production collectively; private property would be abolished; the state would wither away since it would no longer be needed to keep the workers in check; and the exploiting classes themselves would disappear. In the transition to communism there would be a socialist phase that would require a dictatorship of the proletariat to keep the former rulers from returning to power. The whole process would be a violent revolutionary one.[2]

It is his vision that lies at the foundation of communist society. Since Marx never saw his dream come true in his own lifetime, he could not foresee the conditions that determined the actual creation of socialism nor the emergence of national leaders like Lenin, Mao, and Tito who would reinterpret his theory and put their own stamp on various national revolutions. Marx was the prophet of the overthrow of capitalism, but his vision of the new society was vague. He knew that social change would come about from the dialectical interaction between economic and technological change and would result in socialism. But Marx's anti-utopianism made him pass over the nature of the new society.[3] So in this century as communist societies were being established, the political movements that were forging the new institutions knew more about what they were abolishing than what they were creating.

Since liberal democratic co-ops which upheld private property, supported the marketplace and co-existed with capitalism were often anti-communist, it was inevitable that Marxist co-ops would try to be substantially different.

Communist co-ops have three distinct characteristics. First, they are revolutionary in both concept and practice. They result from a violent upheaval in a society and they are used in the post-revolutionary period as a tool to attack capitalism and its proponents and to create new forms of production and exchange. Second, they are always state-initiated, promoted, and maintained as compared to the voluntary nature of liberal democratic co-ops. When decreed they are usually made universal in scope so as to encompass the whole sector to which they apply. They were not presented as an 'alternative' among other options but as the correct and often only way of doing things. Third, communist co-operatives are part of a centrally planned and government-controlled economic system. Although the nature of that planning and control varies from one communist society to another (sometimes considerably), the basic structure is directed toward planning rather than the marketplace.

Because of their deeply engrained opposition to private property and personal profit from the labour of others, communist co-operatives are basically collectives. A collective is a grouping in which control or owner-ship or decision-making is the prerogative of the whole collective. People live together or work together on a collective basis with their livelihood dependent not on private resources or assets but on those of the group. Augmenting this collective reality is the powerful presence of the state and the ruling communist party, which plays such a determining factor in all social and economic relations. The following description captures the basic thrust of communist collectives:

> In all Communist countries, the greatest possible emphasis has been placed throughout on economic growth and development, notably of the industrial sector, which was in some cases minimal when the Communists took over. But it was also taken for granted from the beginning that this economic development must occur under the auspices of the state, one of whose absolutely prime functions it was to plan and organize this enterprise and to take all necessary measures for the purpose, including in many cases coercion of un-willing populations.[4]

In this chapter we will be be discussing three examples of the Marxist tradition. The first and oldest is the Union of Soviet Socialist Republics; the second is the Peoples' Republic of China and the third is the Socialist Federal Republic of Yugoslavia. Each of these countries has a unique form of collective organization. In Russia it is the kolkhoz. In China it is the commune. In Yugoslavia it is the system of workers self-management. These collectives are not only different from each other, but more im-portantly, they have been developed explicitly in opposition to each other as a kind of rejection or denunciation of another communist country's view of what is the correct form of socialist organization.

In spite of the fact that each of these three countries calls itself Marxist and is ruled by a Communist Party that came to power by revolutionary war; in spite of the fact that they have developed a similar state apparatus and centrally administered economy, they view themselves as ideological foes. Their indigenous national traditions, based on their own historical experiences, have pushed through the general outlines of Marxism to create their own forms of anti-capitalist social and economic organization. It is the interplay of Marxist ideology with the historical conditions and traditions unique to each of these countries that has generated variety in communist co-ops.

RUSSIA AND THE KOLKHOZ

Russia at the time of the Revolution (1917-1921) was a vast empire, the largest nation in the world and one that was predominantly peasant.[5] By European standards, Russia was a backward country whose serfs had been freed from their feudal obligations only fifty years earlier. Although in the twenty years prior to World War I, there had been moves toward modernization via the constitutionalization of the autocratic monarchy and through some industrialization, Russian capitalism was basically underdeveloped and the Russian nobility and gentry retained important power.

It was in this context that Lenin's Bolsheviks led the world's first successful communist revolution. They waged a four-year civil war against the old regime and various other political opponents and with their victory they set about creating a new society. In the first years, policy fluctuated as the Party consolidated its power while meeting the immediate needs of a country devastated by war, but eventually the main outline of the communist approach appeared. In the cities the socialization of the means of production meant the abolition of private ownership of industry, severe restrictions on the marketplace, state ownership, planning and control. Since Marxism was a working class ideology, the Russian communists felt they had a firm handle on industry through nationalization and on politics through the dictatorship of the proletariat. Co-operatives of the liberal democratic kind were instituted to provide consumer services for urban workers, but these were nationalized in the mid-thirties. In rural areas the situation was allowed to drift until 1929 because the Marxists were uncertain about how to reconcile the peasant's desire for land with the party's desire to place all production under state control.

Before their rise to power, the Russian communists under Lenin had already indicated a basic distrust and animosity toward the peasantry. The main leftwing enemies of the Bolsheviks were the Social Revolutionaries, a party that represented the populist current in Russian politics. They were firmly based in the countryside and maintained a pro-peasant viewpoint. Their ideology promoted an indigenous Russian socialism based on the communal practices of the rural village (the mir). The Bolsheviks rejected this as a backward view and as true Marxists considered the peasantry to be subservient to the needs of the workers' state. They wanted modernization, industrialization, and socialization and they viewed the peasantry as an obstacle to this process.[6]

'On Co-operation' was the title of Lenin's last major work prior to his death in 1924. He definitely saw a role for co-operatives in agriculture but none in industry. He envisaged a network of co-operatives that would completely encompass agricultural production. He felt membership could be voluntary because the economic benefits of the co-ops would attract peasant participation. Since Lenin did not give co-ops a role in industrial production, one can conclude that he considered co-ops as a rudimentary form of socialist organization.[7] His views, however, were not the determining factor. In the power struggle that followed Lenin's death, Stalin became the dominant force and he fashioned the new form of co-operative that was to characterize Russian agriculture for decades.

Up to 1929, 97 percent of Soviet agricultural production was private.[8] There were some small collective farms with an average of twelve households each, some communes, and some state farms.[9] In 1930 collective forms of consumption were prohibited and communes were abolished. The peasant population was forced into collective production (with private consumption) through the kolkhoz, or collective farm. The only other option for a peasant was the sovhoz, or state farm, in which he was a salaried employee. In one brief six month period, the percentage of peasant households in collective farms went from 4 to 56 percent.[10]

Theoretically, the kolkhoz was a co-operative organization which peasants joined voluntarily in order to farm collectively. The surplus or profit from production was to be divided among the members and they were allowed a few animals and a small private plot for themselves. In practice, the kolkhoz was imposed on the peasants in a campaign of confiscation, incarceration, deportation, and famine. Estimates range from three to thirteen million dead in the collectivization.[11] The following quote from the preamble to the Kolkhoz Model Charter of 1935 accurately depicts the spirit of the collectivization campaign:

> The toiling peasants of the village......of the district of......voluntarily band together into an agricultural artel [kolkhoz] in order to establish with common means of production and with organized common labor, a collective, i.e. a joint farm, to ensure complete victory over the kulaki [rich peasants], over all exploiters and enemies of the toilers, over want and ignorance, over the backwardness of small individual farming, to create high productivity of labor and by this means to ensure the well-being of the members.

The path of collective farming, the path of socialism, is the only right path for the toiling peasants. The members of the artel take upon themselves the obligation to strengthen their artel, to work honestly, to distribute the collective farm income according to the amount of work done, to guard the common property, to take care of the collective farm property, to keep the tractors and machinery in good order, to tend the horses carefully, to execute the tasks imposed by the workers and peasants government in order to make their bolshevik collective farm and all its members prosperous.[12]

The kolhoznik could not leave the collective farm freely; there was no secret ballot in voting; collective work was paid at year end in proportion to the number of 'labour-days' worked and this was most often in kind, at least up to the mid-Fifties.[13] Since it was government policy to purchase agricultural products at artificially low prices, the kolhoz had little if any surplus to distribute. The kolhoznik survived on his meagre private plot (most often worked by his wife) and his few animals which he was able to sell at 'market' prices. The impact on agriculture was devastating. It was not until the 1970s, that peasant consumption reached 1927 levels![14]

The reasons why Soviet agriculture adopted this particular form of organization is still a matter of debate. In the 1920s before Stalin took absolute control, there were Bolsheviks who argued that what was needed was a moderate approach in which surplus agricultural production could be enticed from the peasantry by the provision of consumer goods, while other Bolsheviks argued that industrialization could be achieved only on the backs of the unwilling peasants through artificially low prices.[15] Since Russia was no longer part of the international movement of capital it had to generate its own surplus for investment, which it did through a policy of low pay to workers, high prices for consumer goods, and low prices to agricultural producers. Funds for investment came from the surplus that the state was able to extract from these various sectors since there was little taxation. Since the state set all prices in this economic plan it designated where the surplus would come from. The provision of private garden plots and animals was a method of keeping the peasant alive, when collective production would not.

In the late Twenties there had been several food requisition campaigns for the cities but the peasants would not co-operate because of low state prices. So collectivization was seen as a way of bringing them in line and preventing the rise of an influential and successful peasant elite (the rich peasant or kulak). The kolkhoz's main objective was to fulfill production and delivery quotas set by the state. Once this was achieved and payment made at official prices, any collective products that remained were either bought by the state at a higher price or distributed to the peasants to feed their animals, since they could not produce fodder on their small plots. The peasant lived with his family in his own house and was responsible for his own income.

The kolkhoz has remained a permanent feature of Russian society but it has evolved in the fifty years since it was instituted. The first historic trend has been an increase in size. In 1938 the average kolkhoz was made up of seventy-eight households, but thirty years later it was five times the size.[16] In 1937 the average kolkhoz had 3,000 acres; by 1953 it was 10,000.[17] The second tendency is for the number of kolkhoz to decrease. Between 1940 and 1969 the number of collective farms decreased from 236,900 to 34,700.[18] The increase in size along with a concomitant decrease in number is also characteristic of agriculture in capitalist countries, but what was unique in Russian agriculture was the third tendency—an increase in the number and size of state farms at the expense of the collective farms. In 1940 there were 4,159 state farms in the Soviet Union cultivating 7.7 percent of the total sown area, while in 1978 there were 20,500 state farms cultivating 51.2 percent of the total sown area.[19] In 1953, 83.9 percent of sown land was kolkhoz; but in 1978 it had dropped to 44.2 percent. These statistics indicate the decline of the kolhoz as a factor in Soviet agriculture. During this period the private sector land has remained constant at about 3 percent.[20]

What is the reason for these trends? In Soviet thinking, the kolkhoz was considered a hybrid that stood between private property and state farms. Yet the direction of socialism, as viewed by Russian Marxists, was toward the ideological purity represented by state enterprise. This view was translated into material support for the state farm because it was a model of communist society, while the kolkhoz received less. The salared employee of the state farm did have quotes to fill collectively, but he was still paid, and his income was not dependent on artificially low prices for agricultural produce. The kolhoznik relied on these unfair prices for his income.

In the post-Stalin period, first under Khrushchev and then Brezhnev, agriculture finally became a priority and payment for produce started to meet the actual costs of production. Rural incomes took an upward turn.[21] In the Fifties roughly 16 percent of total Soviet investment was in agriculture but in the Seventies it had increased to 25 percent.[22] This was achieved by having the kolkhoz resemble more closely the operations of a state farm. In 1969 a new charter was promulgated for the kolkhoz and a system of wages was introduced. So not only was there a historical trend to diminish the importance of the kolkhoz but the kolkhoz that remained were being modeled more and more closely after the state farm.

Was this simply a recognition of the failure of the kolkhoz to fit into the Soviet system? In part it was, but more significantly the downgrading of the kolkhoz marked the end of the period of emphasis on industrialization. By the Sixties the Soviet Union had its industrial infrastructure in place and rather than having a need for investment funds wrung from agriculture it needed more food. In this new period it was not that Soviet government looked more kindly on the collective farm but that it came to treat it as a state farm. The sovhoz had been well integrated into the central planning process because it was a form of factory whose input and output fit a command economy. The collective farm as a model of co-operation did not fit as well as the factory farm.

The kolkhoz was the first model of a Marxist co-operative and it epitomized the three basic characteristics mentioned at the beginning of this chapter. It was born after a revolutionary war; it was created by government decree and it was made subservient to a centrally planned economy. As a tool of class struggle, it was aimed at the elimination of the better-off peasants and was used to support the working-class goal of industrialization without foreign investment. Marxist hostility to the peasantry meant that party leaders incorporated that spirit into their approach. Communism could tolerate the peasant's desire for individual production and ownership when it was expedient but it considered that attitude anti-socialist and one that it could not allow to spread.

The concept of a self-governing autonomous unit such as a liberal democratic co-op is quite different from the kolkhoz which had to fit a nonmarket economy. The two-price system devised for the kolkhoz did not work as an incentive. Only the private plot did. It was not so much that the private plot worked because it was 'private' but because it was crucial to survival and because prices for its products (milk and eggs) were often as much as ten times official prices. It is interesting to note that once workers were able to have their own garden plots and increased prices and wages came into effect, kolkhoz family income from the private plot fell from 36 percent of total income in 1965 to 25 percent in 1978.[23]

In a planned economy certain sectors and constituencies are supported or attacked. The kolkhoz has been shown to be a weak institution in such a system because it was created to serve the interests of others. The collective farm did not give power and independence to those who lived and worked in it. As a subordinate class in Marxist thought, the Russian peasantry was forced into the kolkhoz to serve a political will and economic goals that were not of its own choosing nor in its interests. The Russian model of co-operation has shown itself to be inferior to the state farm, not because it is inherently inferior but because the system was against it. The history of the kolkhoz shows that the contradictions and restrictions with which it was saddled meant that it would end up being a transitory phenomenon precisely as the theory viewed it.

Since Marxism did not provide a clear model of socialist agriculture, each national communist revolution found itself free to create its own models, nor did it feel bound by any precedents. This was the case with China, whose communist revolution eventually produced its own form of co-operation and so expanded the number of Marxist models.

CHINA AND THE COMMUNE

In 1949, thirty years after the Russian revolution, China's own communist revolution triumphed. Like Russia, China was an agrarian society with 85 percent of its huge population living in the countryside. China's feudal monarchy had been overthrown in 1911, but the republic that came into being was weak and the basic feudal structure persisted among the peasantry until the communist revolution. That revolution also brought the first permanent peace that China had enjoyed in half a century.

China had come under foreign control in the nineteenth century and the foreign powers that held concessions played an important role in the country's historical development. In the 1920s political power was divided among various provincial warlords, the nationalist government of Jiang Jieshi (Chang Kai Shek), which considered itself the legitimate heir of the republic established in 1911, and the communists eventually led by Mao. The communists and the nationalists fought a civil war from 1927 to 1937 and continued it while fighting the Japanese until 1945. The communists then defeated the nationalists and became the government of China in 1949.

Co-operative history in China differs significantly from the Russian experience. While Russia had had some liberal democratic co-operatives prior to the revolution, which persisted until the collectivization of the 1930s, China had no such tradition. It was not until the war with Japan that liberal democratic co-operatives were introduced in any significant way, and when they were, they were introduced by foreigners in China's weakest sector—industry. Nevertheless, the short and limited experience of these co-operatives played a role in the evolution of a distinctly Chinese communist form of co-operation—the commune. Interestingly, Russia had had no experience of industrial co-operation of any significance and that contributed to the its emphasis on state ownership. China developed differently.

The history of Chinese co-operatives begins with the industrial co-ops of World War II and is followed by the co-operativization of agriculture between 1950 and 1957 and then the collectivization from 1957 to 1961 of both industry and agriculture. In each of these phases there was tension between indigenous needs and Marxist theory which eventually resolved itself in an indigenous form of communism.

Chinese Industrial Co-operatives, also known as CIC or Indusco, was launched as a national movement in 1937, the year in which the invading Japanese destroyed 90 percent of China's large-scale industry, which had been concentrated in the major ocean ports and river cities.[24] The idea for creating industrial co-operatives originated with Rewi Alley, a New Zealander who was a factory inspector for the Municipal Council of Shanghai. In the development and promotion of the idea he was assisted by the American journalist Edgar Snow, who became the major interpreter of the Chinese communist experience to the outside world, and by Snow's wife, Nym Wales, herself a journalist. The first industrial co-operative was set up by a group of illiterate refugee blacksmiths and within a year, sixty-nine of these co-ops had been set up. The number peaked in 1941 with 1,867 co-ops, but then declined rapidly to 282 by 1945. In the communist-controlled areas the co-ops were not started until 1942 and by 1946 they had increased to 590.[25]

The Indusco co-ops operated on the Rochdale model. They subscribed share capital; they were completely voluntary; and they distributed profits among the members. They received Chinese government and foreign aid. Two things stand out about Indusco co-ops. First, they operated in both communist and noncommunist parts of China and were approved and promoted by warring ideologies. Second, they got a head start in the noncommunist territory but eventually did better in the communist areas. Nym Wales, in her wartime book describing Indusco, explained that the goals of these co-ops were the building of democracy and industry and also the building of bridges between the nationalists and the communists in the war.[26] The democratic component came from the experience of self-determination and equality that the co-op gave those who had previously experienced only oppression and exploitation. Indusco brought industrial production under local domestic Chinese control and provided a livelihood for refugees. The industrial task consisted of salvaging equipment and laying the basis for the postwar industrialization of China.

The idealistic hopes of its founders are portrayed in this description of Indusco provided by Nym Wales:

> It wanted to create something clean and honest and for the benefit of the workers themselves, a movement that would command the respect and enthusiasm of all the patriotic and disinterested

elements in the country and sympathizers abroad. A project that would enlist support from the best professional and technical talent in China as well as the enthusiastic confidence of the refugees and workers themselves.[27]

Since the nationalist side was supported by both foreign and domestic bourgeoisie, it was inevitable that the industrial co-operative movement would be viewed by them as a threat, but the Japanese invasion made it expedient to lend Indusco support. The same was true of the communists, who were initially lukewarm to the idea, but eventually took it up as part of their united front strategy. Indusco worked for them because it bolstered war production through a series of semi-mobile workshops that produced much needed material.

The spirit that ran through the Indusco co-ops is expressed in this simple statement of one such co-operative's regulations:

Register all transactions
Balance accounts daily
Inside this society all are brothers
There is really no need for many rules
The important thing is to do your duty.[28]

The CIC was the first organization to create new industry in the interior and it founders hoped that it would eventually involve a million people. But the resumption of civil war brought an end to Indusco. When the Chinese took control of their own destiny in 1949, the only foreigners with any influence were the Russians. Writing in 1941, Nym Wales expressed the hope that whether China went capitalist or communist, "co-operative industry would form a democratic base for whatever form of government emerged."[29] This hope was eventually realized in that the Chinese Communists developed a more popularly based system of collectives than had the Russians. The experience of twenty years of guerilla warfare meant that the principles of decentralization, self-help, and local initiative so crucial to survival became part of the viewpoint of the leadership. The Indusco model was not all that far removed from what the Chinese attempted in the late fifties in the Great Leap Forward and the commune. Since Indusco dealt primarily with industry it never touched the vast agrarian reality of China, and since it was foreign-initiated it was suspect. Once the Japanese had been defeated the impetus for these co-ops dissipated. It was left to the Chinese to create their own model of co-operation.

In 1951 the Chinese Communist government introduced land reform, which involved the confiscation of landlords' holdings and their redistribution among poor peasants. Since these peasants now had land but no equipment or animals, the government encouraged the formation of mutual aid teams that pooled resources for harvesting, etc. The government then initiated a central state-run purchasing and marketing system and encouraged the formation of producer co-ops among the peasants. By the mid-Fifties sixty percent of China's 110 million households belonged to these "semi-socialist agricultrual producer co-ops."[30] These co-ops were very small in size and were based on twenty to thirty households.

In communist strategy co-operatives are part of the transition to a true socialist society. They are used to undermine private property through socialization of production and distribution, thereby laying the groundwork for collectivization. On July 31 1955 Mao delivered his speech "On the Co-operative Transformation of Agriculture" which was to launch a speed-up in the co-operativization of agriculture through the formation of what were called "higher-level" co-ops. These advanced co-ops were modeled on the kolkhoz and were meant to equalize both resources and income among peasants and to increase the size of the unit of production. In a single year 96 percent of peasant households were enrolled.[31] In these advanced co-ops not only were labour and tools pooled but the land was collectively owned and managed with remuneration on the basis of how much one worked. The co-ops had to meet state-negotiated production norms. Rene Dumont, an international authority on the agricultural practices of communist countries, considers the Chinese collectivization to be much less brutal than the Soviet one.[32] This conclusion is confirmed by other Western observers.[33]

The advanced co-op was an intermediate step but an important one. It added velocity to the process of collectivization. The Chinese were not satisfied with the earlier producer co-ops because their size "hampered the development of productive forces."[34] The slogan they now promoted was "The Bigger the Co-operative, the Greater the Superiority." Secondly, they made an increase in production the standard of success. As Mao wrote, "The main criteria by which every co-operative judges whether it is socialist is to see whether its production is rising and by how much."[35] The ease with which the advanced co-ops were created encouraged the authorities to push further.

In 1958 the Party launched "The Great Leap Forward," a program to bring about a dramatic increase in agricultural and industrial production. Simultaneous with the Great Leap Forward was the transformation of the 740,000 advanced co-ops into 24,000 people's communes. There were on average about thirty advanced co-ops to a commune, which then totalled 5,000 families on a land base of 4,500 hectares.[36] Under the slogan "Communism is paradise and the peoples' communes the ladder on which we can reach it" not only was production completely collectivized but so was consumption.[37] Communal eating facilities were set up and the commune was hailed as a model of self-sufficiency. One observer has written that the Great Leap Forward:

> represented a revulsion against the adoption of foreign ways. This was signalled most clearly by the formation of the people's communes and by the prominence give to development through labour-intensive small industry, the practice of 'sending-down' party and government cadres, staff of enterprises and professional people for spells of manual work...[38]

The commune became the basis of economic, social and administrative life in China. Rural communes industrialized and urban communes began to carry on some agricultural projects. The society worked to overcome the division between urban and rural life. At the time of the Sino-Soviet split in 1958-61, the commune became a symbol as well as the practice which rejected the Russian emphasis on heavy industry as separate from agriculture. The Chinese under Mao turned to the Ya'nan model for their development strategy. Ya'nan (Yenan) was the communist base during a crucial period of the civil war. Here they developed a self-sufficient guerilla economy while encircled by a tight nationalist blockade. Survival depended on ingenuity and self-reliance. Great stress was placed on the power of collective human effort to overcome obstacles.[39]

The commune came as close to a communist utopia as any Marxist model has even come. The commune was ten to twenty times the size of the Russian kolkhoz and it combined agricultural and industrial production, administration, education, and defense. The following is a description of the structure of the Zhengzhou urban people's commune:

> Here a factory became the nucleus of a people's commune which took in the entire surrounding population of 10,500 people. New satellite factories were set up around the core factory to employ dependants and process waste. All commercial and service facilities in the area (formerly run by the city) were now taken over and run by the commune. A 'red and expert' university was set up together with elementary and night schools. The entire neighbourhood was organized into a militia unit and...two agricultural production brigades and one sheep milk station were attached. The keynote was 'self-sufficiency,' not that the agricultural land was expected to feed

43

the entire population but it could at least help.[40]

The basic unit of a commune was the work team, composed of several dozen families, who were most likely related to each other. The teams were then formed into brigades of 800 to 1,000 people and the brigades into a commune. Rene Dumont visited a commune in 1975 which had 43,200 inhabitants (32,000 in 1958). It was divided into twenty-two brigades and 242 workteams employed in both the fields and food processing plants.[41] Remuneration was based on a combination of fulfillment of norms plus work-points which were converted into monetary payment. In addition there was private income from extramural work and private plots.

In the 1960-1962 period China suffered a famine and some of the more extreme aspects of communal life were dropped. By 1961 consumption had returned to the individual household and the commune took on a stabilizing administrative role rather than being an ideological cutting edge. Communes have become "a permanent feature of Chinese rural life" and "the mainstay of China's organizational strategy for agricultural development."[42] They survived the turmoil of the Great Cultural Revolution of the mid-Sixties and they are now part of the legacy of Mao to Chinese communism. Today 80 percent of the Chinese 800 million people—are organized into work teams of twenty to thirty households.

The assessment of the commune's contribution is generally favourable in comparison to the Soviet model. Rene Dumont calls it "an original model of development" and he feels it has worked well for an overpopulated country like China.[43] One expert concludes that the commune allowed China to avoid dependency on the Russians.[44] But the most enthusiastic support for the commune comes from the Third World Marxist economist, Samir Amin. According to him China generated a 3 to 4 percent growth rate over the last thirty-five years, which is a figure "virtually without historical precedence."[45] Its policy of self-sufficiency and a do-it-yourself approach have created sustained growth without dependence on foreign investment. The communal structure has created a high degree of egalitarianism. In China the salary ratio of the lowest to the highest paid worker is 1 to 1.5 or 2, while in Eastern Europe it is 1 to 5 and in capitalist Third World countries it is as much as 1 to 10.[46] Amin sees the commune as "the skeletal form of a worker-controlled and rural-based agroindustrial productive system."[47]

What were the ideological sources of this innovation? The Chinese communists wanted to end the division between worker and peasant, city and country, cadre and people. They insisted on implementing their programs more through group pressure and persuasion than force. They insisted on a populist policy of going to the countryside to learn from the peasants. The Party made its mass appeal on the basis of raising the standard of living of the peasantry. All this came from the guerilla experience of the communists rather than from Marxist theory. When Mao developed his line in the late twenties and early thirties that the peasantry was to be the base of the communist revolution, he was deviating from the Soviet European working-class approach. Mao was adapting to the realities of Chinese society and it was the success of the adaptation that resulted in a Maoist and post-Maoist emphasis on the rural areas. Besides, pragmatism demanded that the feeding of one billion people could only happen with a policy that mobilized the peasantry.

The abandonment of the Soviet model and its emphasis on heavy industry created an alternative development scheme for China. Within the context of the Sino-Soviet split and the battle between the two communist giants for influence in the Third World, the commune became China's offering on how to organize communist societies after a successful revolution.

In spite of the differences with the Soviet model, Chinese collectives retained the three basic characteristics of Marxist co-operatives. They were state-instituted after a revolutionary war and were part of a centrally planned economy. The speed with which they were instituted displayed the power of the Party. The general acceptance of collectivization was due to the Party's close contacts with the peasantry and with the steady evolution from one form of co-operative organization to another. In Russia, there was no such evolution. The New Economic Program, instituted in the 1920s, left agriculture pretty much alone and then abruptly collectivized. Nevertheless there are similarities between Russia and China in the development of co-operatives. First, the time span—1920 to 1929 in Russia and 1949 to 1959 in China—is similar for both countries. It took about ten years in power before they had created the form they wanted. Secondly, both systems were national in scope. It was a single form that dominated the whole country with some regional variations. With the higher level or advanced co-ops of 1955-1956 the Chinese actually went through a kolkhoz stage but that was quickly surpassed in terms of the degree of collectivization by the commune. In a sense, it can be argued that the Chinese went further along the road to communism than the Russians because the kolkhoz has turned out to be an intermediate step on the way to the state farm, while the commune has not been surpassed in China.

Although the commune is waning as an all-encompassing solution in contemporary post-Maoist China, this is not the result of it being an intermediate stage to something more Marxist. It is waning because of

China's retreat from Maoism and the strict reliance on self-development. With a decline in ideological fervor of the kind that fueled Maoist changes and a reintroduction of a private sector, the commune may very well slip from its pedestal. The implications for Chinese communism of such a development can only be assessed in the future.

YUGOSLAVIA AND WORKERS' SELF-MANAGEMENT

Like China, Yugoslavia has developed its own form of co-operative-collective institution during a period of conflict with the Soviet Union. It happened in 1948 when Tito rebuffed Stalin and refused to have Yugoslavia integrated into the Eastern bloc. Tito was the head of the League of Communists and the new Yugoslav republic created by Communist partisans after a four-year war against the German occupation. Until he displayed his independence, Tito like Mao, had been supported by the Russians.

The writer Milovan Djilas, a close associate and later critic of Tito, explained the split with the Soviet Union as "the resistance of Yugoslav communism to Soviet expansion."[48] Because of the split Yugoslavia established a prototype of an independent communist state in Europe. It pursued its own nonalignment foreign policy and internally it developed a unique form of socioeconomic system called workers self-management in order to distinguish itself from Russian communism. A number of Party thinkers, such as Djilas, encouraged Tito to make a break with the Russian style of command economy. Since Yugoslavia was still very much a peasant country, the communists needed a development strategy and Tito agreed to create his own. Djilas has described this innovation of workers' self-management in these terms:

> ...the concept of self-management was born from the struggle against Stalinist tyranny and from visions of a true democratic socialism. Self-management legalized criticism of the bureaucracy. It also suppressed bureaucratic willfulness. And it solidified gains toward a free-market economy...[49]

Djilas pointed out that self-management, while radically different from the Soviet state bureaucratic model, was nonetheless based in Marxism and that it was created by the Communist Party, which continued to retain full political control of the country's development. Self-management never threatened the Party's power nor Tito's pre-eminent leadership. Like the commune in China, workers self-management was hailed by its founders as the only true form of communism and like the commune for China, it became "the most characteristic of Yugoslav institutions" and "the pivotal institution of the Yugoslav socioeconomic system."[50]

Officially promulgated into law in 1950, self-management was a creation of the Party and the state. It has subsequently become enshrined in the Yugoslav constitution. Originally, self-management had its roots in the thinking of utopian socialists of the early nineteenth century such as Fourier, Owen, and Saint-Simon, and its main proponent was Proudhon, another of those condemned by Marx as utopian. If anything, Yugoslavia has shown that self-management is not utopian. As one writer as stated: "the self-management model of socialism is not only theoretically plausible but it is also practically feasible and possible."[51] One has to ask then in what sense self-management is Marxist and communist.

Self-management has three fundamental components. First, it provides for the autonomous management of a firm by councils elected by the workers of the firm. Second, it provides for the existence of a competitive market mechanism for setting prices and ensuring profits. Third, it creates the concept of social property in opposition to state property and makes social property the prime form in the country.

Workers self-management is akin to worker or producer co-ops of the Rochdale kind because it ensures decision-making on a one person/one vote basis in an enterprise that is autonomous in its operation. Several scholars have called self-management "the extension of the co-operative principle."[52]

In his 1950 speech introducing workers self-management, Tito called state ownership the lowest form of socialist ownership and claimed that industry owned and operated by worker councils was the highest form. Yugoslav theorists claim that workers self-management expresses several of Marx's ideas. First, it fits with his idea of the withering away of the state and an economy run by a free association of producers. Second, the direct control by workers over the surplus value that their labour creates is more in line with Marx's view of communism than is state control. And third, Marx's dream of the abolition of the technological division of labour is possible through a work community created by self-management.[53] What self-management is meant to do is to transform sellers of wage-labour into self-regulating producers.

The system has gone through a number of evolutionary stages. In the initial period from 1949 to 1952 workers'councils were basically consultative. From 1953 to 1962 they took on real decision-making power. In 1963 the Yugoslav constitution made self-management the hallmark of a society in which firms competed for profit and growth. The firms are autonomous in setting production targets, investment, prices, and wages and their top managers were elected. All workers in a firm elect by secret ballot a council that manages the company for two years. It meets monthly and is the basic policy-making body. There is also an elected managing board, three-quarters of whom are production workers.[54] In the Sixties self-management rights were transfered to smaller work units to ensure direct democracy.

How has the system fared in its thirty-five years of existence? Yugoslavia has registered one of the most impressive growth rates in the world.[55] However there is a suspicion that the system is limited in terms of real worker participation in decision-making.[56] One factor that may limit participation is the large size of production units. 1978 figures show that firms employing more than 10,000 workers used one-third of the industrial work force in the country.[57] This means that self-management could have as little impact on individual workers as membership voting rights in a large liberal democratic co-op.

Another problem of self-management is 'market socialism,' the system by which firms compete with for labour and sales. Yugoslavia has had a steadily increasing rate of unemployment. In 1955 it stood at three percent and twenty years later it was ten percent.[58] Large-scale emigration has been used to try to solve the problem of surplus labour with limited success. Yugoslavia's independent path has tied its economy more to the capitalist West than the communist East and has made it susceptible to capitalist cycles. To offset market pressures for wage differentials the government has tried to ensure equality through social programs and significant industrial planning and the creation of firms where it feels they are most needed. The government's view is that the system of market socialism encourages co-operation among various firms because the ethic of self-management is one of social responsibility rather than private profit. A survey of wage earners showed that three-quarters of workers, two-thirds of office staff, and one-half of supervisors felt that income differentials should not exceed a ratio of 1 to 3.[59] This would incate that the government had succeeded in promoting an egalitarian ideology.

During the Fifties both Russia and China denounced Yugoslavian self-management as revisionist and noncommunist. Nevertheless, the Yugoslav system does fulfill the three basic characteristics of communist collectives: it was created after a revolutionary war; it was created by the state and became a national policy; and finally it is dominated by a planned economy. This latter characteristic is not as pronounced as that of Russia or China, but it is still very much there in the sense that the government monitors the economy closely, guides new development firmly, and intervenes whenever it thinks it is necessary. The lack of any significant private sector, the universality of the self-management system, and the presence of an all-pervasive communist party ensures state dominance.

Yugoslavia has achieved an impressive degree of decentralization and in economic matters it has devolved more decision-making power to ordinary workers than any other communist state. One author has referred to self-management as the re-emergence of the "Partisan ethic," which would approximate Mao's emphasis on a guerilla-style economy of the Ya'nan model.[60] Yugoslavia differs from China and Russia in making its collective innovation in industry rather than in agriculture. Yet like China it favours decentralization, though of a different sort than that represented by the commune.

Self-management is a form of communist collective that is as different from the commune and the kolkhoz as those two are from each other. In this it confirms the ability of communist societies and leaderships to develop co-operative forms of organization that can reflect different national cultures and traditions, that can be placed comfortably into a Marxist ideological framework, and that can fulfill the need of states to have a distinct socio-economic identity. It should not be forgotten that the two communist countries—China and Yugoslavia—that developed their own forms of socio-economic organization were two that, like Russia, had carried out their revolution with little outside support.

THE IDEOLOGY OF COMMUNIST COLLECTIVES

In spite of their differences and the practice of communist countries to denounce each other's deviation from true Marxism, communist collectives share a basic ideology and the contradictions which flow from it.

First, Marxist ideology is based on the rejection of the exploitative use of the means of production for personal profit. It opposes private property and the capitalist marketplace because they create inequality and injustice. Second, communism has adopted a state-directed economic system to replace private enterprise and the marketplace and it has turned to collective forms of economic production. Third, Marxism teaches that communism, the stage at which every one will receive according to his or her needs, must be preceded by a socialist phase, in which each receives according to his labour.[61] Communist government have always argued that the lack of material abundance precludes the establishment of full communism and necessitates the continuation of society at the socialist level. Marxist governments invariably call their societies socialist and their parties communist. The former expresses their achievement while the latter expresses their goals. Fourth, Marxism states that the socialist phase requires a dictatorship of the proletariat to protect the revolution against a return to capitalism. This dictatorship has been the justification for permanent party rule and has legitimized the Party's right to determine and impose those socio-economic forms that it feels are appropriate.

How does the operation of communist collectives compare with liberal democratic co-operatives? First liberal democratic co-ops are well-established within the capitalist system, whose commitment to private property and the marketplace they firmly uphold. Communist collectives, while viewing themselves as democratic, are anticapitalist. They are as devoted to the prerogatives of the Party and the state as liberal democratic ones are to their members. One Chinese text states that relations between co-ops "must be in accordance with the state plan and have approval of the leading organ."[62] Second, liberal democratic co-ops are voluntary. One can enter and leave them as the need arises, whereas communist collectives are only nominally voluntary. Nonparticipation is penalized, whether through group pressure or the law. Third, liberal democratic co-ops see their development as a gradual, evolutionary process, while communist collectives are part of a revolutionary process. This process is one of class warfare, in which liberal democratic co-ops do not engage. Fourth, liberal democratic co-ops require only a minimal level of involvement, while communist collectives are much more all-encompassing. Fifth, liberal democratic co-ops portray themselves as non-partisan politically, while communist collectives emphasize party leadership, the task of building socialism, and the need for enthusiasm and commitment to ideology, none of which is part of the Rochdale model. And finally, the communist collectives are much more attuned to production than to consumption, while the reverse is true of liberal democratic co-ops.

What the two systems share is the reality of variation and differences within each system. Neither Rochdale-style co-operatives nor communist collectives are monolithic and uniform. At the same time the principles that underline each system remain, and those systems continue to be loyal to their underlying beliefs. It is interesting to note that both co-op systems began as anti-capitalist movements. The liberal democratic one adapted, while the communist collectives used a strong and ruthless revolutionary government to defeat an equally strong and ruthless capitalism. Both share the goal of improving the conditions of the dispossessed, but which tradition has been 'more successful' in achieving that goal requires a case by case evaluation which is beyond the scope of this book.

Nevertheless, it is worthwhile to discuss the contradictions of communist collectives as we did in the previous chapter for liberal democratic co-ops. The first contradiction is between the workers and the state. The Chinese text quoted previously claims that "socialist public ownership is the negation of all exploitative systems...[and] that surplus value is at the service of the labouring classes."[63] The communist ideal is that the workers benefit equally from their work, but other than in the Yugoslav system, members of communist collectives have little control over the disposal of the surplus value they produce. Since the state takes most of the surplus value and uses it according to its own priorities, workers and peasants can justly complain that they have been individually exploited for the national good, which includes hundreds of millions of other individuals with which they may not identify.

Second, there is the contradiction between the working class orientation of Marxism and the fact that in most cases it has triumphed in poor peasant societies that are severely underdeveloped. This theoretical handicap has meant that communist collectives have developed agriculture along factory lines and have treated farmers as workers, which goes against their traditional small producer interests.

Third, there is the contradiction between the communist emphasis on idealistic incentives and the need for material rewards at the socialist stage. Workers ought to be motivated by communist values but communist collectives have had to use material incentives to increase production. This had caused income differentials and class stratification.

Fourth, there is the contradiction between the goal of eliminating the state and the reality of authoritarian and dictatorial Marxist governments. Collectives which were meant to express the flowering of human co-operation have been imposed from on high, thereby perpetuating a powerful state mechanism which Marxism hoped to end.

Contradictions between theory and practice cannot be considered something bad in themselves. They are in fact the driving force of history. The achievement of ideal conditions would mean an end to the historical process as such, and that is an absurdity. It is the struggle to realize ideals and the resulting failure that provides material for further development and evolution. Using communist collectives, Marxist societies have made notable economic progress. The Soviet Union has risen to major power status and China has replaced Japan as the pre-eminent regional power in Asia. The fact that China has been able to feed its vast population adequately for the first time in centuries is of credit to the revolution and that Yugoslavia has the greatest degree of worker self-management in the world is no mean achievement for democracy in the workplace.

In comparing co-operatives in capitalist countries and collectives in communist ones, one is struck by the fact that neither has reached its ideals. In the case of liberal democratic co-ops that goal is the end of capitalism, and in the case of Marxist collectives the goal is the creation of pure communism. The failure to reach these goals provides a historical incentive to each tradition to continue to develop in the effort to overcome its present limitations.

Chapter Four:
THE SOCIALIST TRADITION

A DEFINITION

Since countries led by communist parties call themselves socialist and liberal democratic co-operatives have roots in utopian socialism, it is necessary to distinguish what I call the socialist tradition from the Marxist and liberal democratic traditions. The most important feature of socialist co-operatives is their having been created by non-Marxist socialist ideologies and by noncommunist political movements. Second, socialist co-ops do not result from government initiatives the way communist collectives do, even though they may be state-supported. Third, socialist co-ops do not arise out of a revolutionary war. They evolve more or less peacefully within a capitalist framework.

These features distinguish socialist co-ops from the Marxist tradition and ally them with the liberal democratic one. So how are socialist co-ops different from the Rochdale ones? First, they maintain a strenuous internal opposition to private property and capitalist practices. Second, they are invariably multifunctional in their services as compared to the one-dimensional nature of liberal democratic co-ops. In short they are full co-operative communities operating on socialist principles in a non-socialist environment. Ideologically, socialist co-ops occupy a middle ground between communist collectives and liberal democratic co-ops.

The socialist co-ops that will be examined in this chapter are well-established systems in their native countries. They are vigorous, dynamic, and well-known components of their societies. Unlike the communes of the communal tradition to be discussed in the next chapter, socialist co-ops are not isolationist. They have strong indigenous roots that distinguish them from the other socialist co-ops in the tradition. This reflection of a particular culture and place limits their transferability. The kibbutz is found only in Israel, but credit unions exist around the world.

The general characteristics of socialist co-ops appear in varying degrees in each kind of co-op. For example, the communal and egalitarian aspects of the kibbutz surpass anything found in communist collectives, while the ujamaa villages of Tanzania are state-initiated and dependent. They are grouped in this chapter because they share most, if not all, of the characteristics and because they fit better in this category rather than others. The differences among socialist co-ops, however, are as great as those in the Marxist tradition.

As we examine these co-ops in detail, one aspect will stand out above all others: their socialism has always gone hand in hand with another forceful ideology. In the case of Israel that ideology is Zionism; in Tanzania it is anti-colonialism and in Mondragon it is Basque nationalism. Although nationalism has played a role in both Communist and liberal democratic co-ops nowhere has it shared such a fundamental partnership as in indigenous socialist co-ops. In this chapter we will be examining the kibbutzim of Israel, the ujamaa villages of Tanzania and the worker co-operative complex at Mondragon in the Basque country of Spain.

Traditionally, socialism has been associated with state ownership and centralized planning. But as one commentator has written, "there are other socialist traditions and habits of thinking. which emphasize the importance of community..."[1] This is the main feature of the agro-industrial co-operative communities of Israel known as kibbutzim. Menachem Gerson, a life-long resident of a kibbutz and a student of its structure, describes a kibbutz as a socialist community that manages its affairs by direct democracy. The means of production are owned and operated by the members of the community and their needs are provided by the community in equal measure for all.[2] In existence for over seventy years the kibbutz has developed an international profile and is probably the most studied of all socialist co-operatives.

The kibbutz is a co-operative because its production and consumption is organized on a democratic basis. It is completely voluntary and all members are equal stakeholders in the enterprise. As a co-operative community it provides housing, education, and medical care for its members. Kibbutz socialist ideology has been described as "a protest against the market mentality...and a movement toward an egalitarian human community."[3] Launched by Zionist pioneers in Palestine prior to World War I, the kibbutz has become a unique and highly successful form of socialism. Since the Israeli economy is a mixed economy in which the marketplace is matched in influence by a strong labor movement, a large public sector, and numerous liberal democratic co-operatives, the kibbutzim have been able to evolve in a supportive environment. They have formed a powerful network of communities fully integrated into the national economy and its political process. This network is considered one of the bulwarks of Israeli society.

The second kind of socialist co-operative community that will be examined is the ujamaa village of Tanzania. Launched shortly after the independence of the country in the 1960s, the ujamaa villages were initiated by Julius Nyerere, President of Tanzania and the head of the ruling political party. 'Ujamaa' is a Swahili word meaning 'familyhood.' The word is meant to express an indigenous African sense of socialism. Nyerere explained it this way:

> By the use of the word 'ujamaa,' therefore, we state that for us socialism involves building on the foundation of our past, and building also to our own design. We are not importing a foreign ideology into Tanzania and trying to smother our distinct social patterns with it.[4]

Nyerere envisaged his country being built on an egalitarian, co-operative and non-acquisitive ideology of its own creation in which no person would use his wealth to exploit others. Unfortunately, the ujamaa village idea did not attract sufficient interest on a voluntary basis so it was eventually imposed on the population with the result that this kind of co-operative community has been the least successful of all socialist co-ops. Even so, it represents the boldest and most far-reaching attempt to create an indigenous form of socialism in post-colonial Africa.

The third example of a socialist co-op is the complex of co-operatives centred on the town of Mondragon in the Basque region of Spain. Launched in the mid-Fifties as a single worker co-operative, Mondragon has grown to encompass over 100 industrial enterprises and sixty other co-ops including 114 branches of the Working People's Bank (Caja Laboral Popular), sixty-three outlets of a consumer co-op, a social insurance system, a technological research centre and engineering school, and various housing, educational, and service coops. It is the largest integrated worker co-operative system in the world.

Ordinarily, one would list worker co-operatives under the liberal democratic tradition because they operate on basic Rochdale principles. But Robert Oakeshott, a contemporary British proponent of worker co-ops, has made the valid point that the liberal democratic designation is appropriate for isolated worker co-ops in a capitalist system, but it does not apply to a complete system such as developed at Mondragon, which has created an institutionalized reality as extensive as self-management in Yugoslavia and the kibbutz in Israel. [5] He states that ''...the kind of socialism which a Mondragon sector would encourage...consists of a self-reliant solidarity between groups of workers of all kinds who share a direct and very real interest in the success of their enterprise.''[6] The co-ops in the Mondragon group exist in eighty-six towns and cities in the region and they operate on Rochdale principles. Yet they are not unifunctional or segmented, but instead have combined their services to create a socialist environment. The percentage of Basques (4%) associated with Mondragon co-ops is similar to the percentage of Israel's Jewish population living in kibbutzim (3%). These figures indicate that both Mondragon and the kibbutzim have attracted a sufficient population to make them movements of world-class stature.

Because Mondragon has gone beyond being a simple worker co-op, its classification as a socialist community is acceptable and will become clearer with a review of its historical and ideological development. Included in this chapter is a discussion of worker co-ops in the U.K., the United States, and in Canada.

Peter Jay describes a worker co-op as a business enterprise in which the ownership of the assets is vested in the members collectively and in which the sovereign body is the members having one vote each and in which employees and only employees are members.[7] The role of worker-owner goes beyond the normal capitalist employment practices of liberal democratic co-ops. Since the worker co-op movement has been a fringe element in a scene dominated by consumer and agricultural producer co-ops, it has been more radical in its ideology. Daily relations in a worker co-op are more intense than those usually found in liberal democratic co-ops.

Yet the fact remains that worker co-ops are essentially unifunctional liberal democratic co-ops in spite of the 'community of the workplace.' Mondragon has shown that this need not be the case. It points clearly to the underdeveloped and very limited socialism of isolated worker co-ops.

ISRAEL AND THE KIBBUTZ

In 1909, a half-dozen Jewish agricultural labourers in Palestine went on strike against their Jewish employer. The main result of the strike was his handing over a swampy part of his land to the group to farm communally. This became the world's first kibbutz (the word comes from the Hebrew 'kvutzah' meaning group).

The labourers were young European Jews who had come to Palestine as Zionists and socialists to participate in the colonization of the country and the creation of a new Jewish society. The major problem they faced in Palestine was unemployment. Arab landowners would not employ them and Jewish landowners preferred to hire Arabs because they cost less and were more accustomed to working in the climate. According to one scholar, only 10 percent of the 10,000 young Jews who came to Palestine between 1904 and 1914 found work.[8] Many returned to Europe.

Although the need for employment was a basic reason for the formation of kibbutzim, another important motivation was ideological. Current at the time was a belief that manual labour and the agrarian way of life was necessary for the regeneration of the Jewish people. A key proponent of this view was Aaron David Gordon, one of the founders of the first kibbutz at Degania and author of Land and Work. Linked to this was the Zionist strategy of creating a Jewish state through settlement. The kibbutz was seen as a good way of encouraging frontier settlements where there was no Jewish presence. Besides agrarianism and Zionism, the kibbutzim reflected European ideas of socialism.

The first kibbutzim were associated with European-based Zionist youth movements, which fueled these experiments by sending members. Prior to the First World War, a kibbutz would have anywhere from five to ten members. It was located on desolate land and its members were known for the hardship they had to endure. Disease, disillusionment, and death were constant companions. While the original kibbutz at Degania had forty-three members by the mid-Twenties, over 300 others had worked there and left.[9] By 1930 there were several thousand adherents and the average kibbutz size was sixty-seven.[10] Today over 100,000 Jews representing 3.5 percent of the non-Arab population live in 260 kibbutzim that produce 35 percent of Israel's agricultural production and 7 percent of its industrial output.

When several dozen kibbutzim formed a federation in the mid-Twenties, they described the kibbutz as a small community based on economic co-operation, the holding of property in common, democratic management of work, collective rearing of children, and the distribution of goods on an egalitarian basis. These principles are the foundation of one of the great success stories of co-operative living in this century. Even though the percentage of the population living in kibbutzim has declined from a peak of about 8 percent in the late Forties and early Fifties, the movement has remained a fundamental feature of Israeli society.

Initially everything was arranged on an *ad hoc* basis and kibbutz society evolved by implementing socialist principles. There was no charismatic individual to lead, only collective enthusiasm. Anyone wishing to join had to agree to communal living arrangements and equality in work and consumption. The kibbutz stood for self-labour and unqualified mutual responsibility in accordance with the communist principle of each according to his ability and to each according to his need. The following model rules for kibbutzim promulgated in the 1930s express the basic thrust of the community:

> The general objects of the society are to organize and promote the social interests of its members in accordance with co-operative principles and in particular to:
>
> a. manage and develop a collective farm...
> c. organize various industries in the settlement
> d. maintain a common purse into which all the earnings of their members shall be paid and from which all their requirements shall be provided.
> e. to assist members in raising their economic, cultural, and social level by mutual aid and to care for their sick, to support the old and feeble and other persons dependent on deceased members, and to maintain and educate the children of members...
> g. to establish and maintain in the settlement public institutions and services and generally undertake all activities which are customarily undertaken by village authorities.[12]

Constructed in a defensive compound style, the kibbutz provided separate living quarters for adults and for children. The children were raised primarily by kibbutz workers and communal eating facilities were the norm. These customs evolved from practical considerations as much as from ideology. In many cases poverty and survival demanded these norms. Eventually four separate federations were incorporated—three secular and one religious. Rather than exist as islands in a sea of private property and capitalism, they formed a series of interconnected cells. Their very size gave them critical mass. As Darin-Drabin has written: "The kibbutzim have reached a greater degree of independence from their capitalist environment than other communes in the capitalist world because none of the latter has so much weight in the national economy..."[13] The federations aligned themselves with various political parties and the powerful trade union movement, which has given them substantial leverage in the country. The links between trade unionism and the kibbutzim are a reflection of the socialist tradition that underlies both.

For forty years the kibbutzim developed in a semi-feudal country controlled first by Turkey and then Britain. As frontier settlements, they were engaged in ongoing conflicts with the Palestinian Arabs. In their second forty years they have been part of a new state that has existed in perpetual war readiness. Because of its colonizing role and its frontier location, the kibbutzim have been closely integrated with the political history of Zionism and the military history of Israel.

This integration was accomplished through three major institutions: the Jewish Agency, the Jewish National Fund, and the Histadrut. The Agency organized emigration and settlement; the Fund purchased land and leased it to the kibbutzim; and the Histadrut organized the members of the kibbutz into a national trade union movement that also spawned many liberal democratic co-ops. During the period of the British Mandate, 35 percent of all Jewish-owned land was owned by the Fund and the Agency provided capital loans for settlements at an interest rate of 2 percent.[14] In all, the Jewish Agency spent 35.9 million pounds on settlements between 1917 and 1945.[15] It was not until the late 1930s that the kibbutzim were able to stop operating on a deficit basis.[16] These figures point out the absolute importance of outside aid in ensuring survival of the kibbutzim.

In the post-independence period outside support remained crucial. In the 1949 to 1965 period 60 percent of outside capital came from world Jewry, 28 percent from German government reparation payments and 12 percent from the United States.[17] This external support enabled the Israeli economy to sustain a high rate of economic investment. The kibbutzim were organized to take maximum advantage of this support. In 1959, with only 4 percent of the population, the kibbutzim cultivated 33 percent of the agricultural land, produced 26 percent of the nation's agricultural output and supplied 25 percent of its rural population.[18]

The kibbutz movement was blessed with a well-developed sense of mission. Its close supportive relationship first with Zionism and then the Israeli state provided economic and political stability. And yet without an efficient communal form of operation, it would have failed. The communal nature of kibbutz life produced economic efficiency in a pioneer setting. The focal points of this communalization are the democratic organization of production, community living, and collective child-rearing and education.

The kibbutzim are basically rural settlements. Supreme authority is vested in the general meeting of all members who have one vote each. Tasks are allocated by elected committees and positions of authority are rotated among members. At any one time, 35 to 40 percent of the members are in charge of some function.[19] After Israeli independence the kibbutzim began to industrialize. Research studies indicate that both kibbutz farms and kibbutz factories are more technologically advanced than their counterparts in the private sector.[20]

The kibbutz guarantees regular employment for all its members and the rotation of people through various offices prevents the accumulation of power in the hands of the few, while the provision of equal economic benefits prevents disparities in wealth. Amia Libelich, in her recent study of the kibbutz, describes kibbutz work culture as emphasizing both manual and mental labour:

> A woman who wrote educational programs for the whole country sits in the laundry room folding sheets...a man who teaches at the kibbutz teacher college sits twice a week on the line in the food factory sorting olives...[21]

In today's kibbutz about 60 percent of the adult members work in the service sector—education, administration, the kitchen and laundry while 40 percent work in the productive branches. Of that 40 percent, two-thirds work in industry and one-third in agriculture.[22]

It is not just formal group ownership that has meaning. The ethos of participation and direct democracy in all activities creates a form of self-management that is unequalled anywhere else. Melford Spiro, an American authority on the kibbutz, explains kibbutz culture as one of "identification with the group, the absence of acquisitive drives, the absence of intense success strivings, a willingness to assume social responsibilities."[23]

When a child is born into the kibbutz its care is divided between the mother and other kibbutz members who are responsible for the care of babies and children. Since the parents work nearby, they have convenient access to their children, but in order to develop identification with the kibbutz the children sleep in their own special quarters. Earlier this provided security for the children during battles with Arabs. Besides this preschool care, the kibbutz provides elementary and secondary education. There is a strong emphasis on education expressed in various study days provided for members, large libraries on most kibbutzim, and post-secondary institutions and publishing houses operated by the federations. The kibbutz aims to provide a complete cultural, economic, and social milieu characteristic of any self-sustaining community. The core of this milieu is work, but the equal sharing of food, housing, clothing, and education ensures the socialist viewpoint.

What are the motivations that would encourage a person to join a kibbutz? Darin-Drabkin has written that kibbutz life appealed to those who were interested in social progress, socialism, and the development of Israel.[24] Every kibbutznik had to have a strong dose of idealism. Golda Meir, the late prime minister of Israel and a kibbutz pioneer, wrote that she was attracted to the kibbutz because it was a "genuine revolutionary social ideal.''[25] One historian of the movement explained that anyone wishing to join had to demonstrate:

> a genuine belief in and a determination to carry out all the basic principles of communitarian living, such as willingness to work, to serve the community to the best of his ability, and also to have a real appreciation of human relationships.[26]

In return for this idealistic motivation, the kibbutz offered a basic form of security in the frontier areas, employment for those out of work, and a social security system backed by the community. In a hostile and undeveloped country like Palestine the provision of food, shelter, and security was important.

Nevertheless conditions were very hard. Some of those who were unable to adjust to the communal way of life spawned two other co-operative forms: the first was the moshav and the second was the shitufi. The first moshav was set up in 1936. It was basically a system of individual family farms grouped around a village community. Goods were purchased and marketed on a co-operative basis. The shitufi were communities that farmed collectively rather than privately but retained a strong family identity in child-rearing. The shitufi is much closer to the kibbutz in operation than the moshav, but it has done away with the communal dining and childrearing of the kibbutz.

Neither the shitufi nor the moshav approach the kibbutz in numbers or influence. In 1973 there were 238 kibbutzim but only thirty-eight moshavim.[27] The main problem that moshavim face is the rule that only one child can inherit the lease on the family farm. And because the moshavim are not industrialized, they are being depopulated like most family farm economies. In spite of their differences, the kibbutz, the moshav, and the shitufi share three basic commitments: no private ownership of land, self-work, and mutual aid.

The kibbutz has faced and continues to face two basic problems: individual adjustment to communal life and kibbutz practices that violate its own basic principles. In the early period there was a very high turnover but by the Fifties this had dropped to an annual rate of less than 10 percent.[28] However in the 1970s the number of young people leaving increased dramatically, so that one authority claims that half of the post-army age youth leave.[29] The lack of a sense of mission that the earlier generation had, the attraction of urban life, and the inability of nonkibbutz spouses to adjust to kibbutz life have contributed to this problem. As the average population of the kibbutzim approaches 500, the sense of a formal social system increases. The kibbutzim have been unable to attract the new immigrants to Israel and so it would seem that for the time being the period of expansion and growth has come to an end.

The kibbutzim have been unable to make substantive progress in removing women from stereotypical roles as child care workers and cooks. But their major internal contradiction has been hired labor. Since the kibbutz is committed to building a classless society within its boundaries, the presence of employees undermines that goal. The kibbutznik is an equal of his peers but a master of other people. The problem arose after the formation of the state, when the Israeli government insisted that the kibbutzim hire people from the large immigration that was flooding into the country. Hired labour is now a common feature of kibbutz life. Kibbutz industries are particularly dependent on hired labour because they have been unable to generate enough manpower from within the kibbutz. The community provides so many social services that a substantial number of its members work in this capacity. As well industrial expansion often requires a block of workers at once to launch an enterprise and yet membership generally does not increase that way.

The Israeli government's insistence that the kibbutzim serve a higher need than their own socialist principle of self-labour points out how the establishment of the state of Israel proved to be a watershed in the evolution of the kibbutz. In the period prior to 1948 the kibbutzim were characterized by their small size and direct interpersonal relations. The kibbutzim were part of a network of voluntary organizations promoting Zionism and they had substantial autonomy in their development. Once independence came the impact of state policies on a minority group like the kibbutzim became overriding. The kibbutzim were large enough to be targetted for a national role but too weak to defend their principles in a head on clash with the state.

After independence the old goals of agricultural colonization and defense of the frontier remained but were integrated into the work of state institutions. The change was subtle but profound. After the creation of the state, the kibbutz, which was patriotic, allowed itself to be directed by nonkibbutz influences. The kibbutz always has had two masters: socialism and Zionism. In the post-independence period it served Zionism first.[30]

Because independence brought a new state of affairs, the kibbutz economy and social organization began to develop in certain directions. First the percentage of the Jewish population living in kibbutzim began a steady decline, though the absolute figure has grown. In spite of this decline, the kibbutz continues to increase its influence in the countryside. In 1961 it made up 25 percent of the rural population. In 1971 it was 33 percent.[31] The result is that the kibbutzim are becoming increasingly important in an ever-diminishing sector of the population.

Second, because of state policy, the kind of agriculture in which kibbutzim engage has moved from self-sufficiency to production for export. This orientation has meant that the kibbutz is even more closely tied to state objectives and needs. This undermines the ability of the kibbutz to develop an independent economic strategy.

Third, the ethnic make-up of the kibbutz represents a diminishing segment of the Jewish population. The European Ashkenazi Jews who founded the kibbutz represent only 48 perecent of the Jewish population today, while the Sephardic Afro-Asian population is now 52 percent and rising. This increasing important element has few political or cultural links with the kibbutz.

Any evaluation of the kibbutz movement must take into account these trends and how they have affected the kibbutz. Many consider the kibbutz as the most successful model of co-operative community in the non-communist world. Among its supporters are those who claim that "the kibbutz experience can serve as proof that societies based on socialistic principles function successfully even when they are surrounded and form part of capitalistic societies."[32] Yet for the kibbutz that functioning has required hired labor in direct contravention of its ideals. The kibbutz shows that "the larger capitalistic society cannot be converted to socialism by small communalistic settlements."[33] The kibbutz never had the power to direct the state along the path of socialist ideals, so it ended up working to create a state that was nonsocialist.

The reason that the kibbutz never went beyond the socialist-cell-in-a-capitalist-world structure was its dual commitment to both socialism and Zionism. In so many ways this combination gave the kibbutz a fundamental strength but in the end one side of this marriage had to dominate and it was nationalism. The failure to move Israeli society toward kibbutz-style socialism meant that the kibbutz was being moved away from its ideals. This has shown itself in the hired labour problem and in the trend away from collective consumption and child-rearing.[34] With 96.5 percent of Jews in Israel not living in kibbutzim, the energy flows against socialism rather than for it.

Melford Spiro described socialism as the universal principle in kibbutz ideology that stood for social and personal liberation and Zionism as the particular principle that stood for national liberation. With the Zionist side the dominant gene and the socialist the recessive one, there are problems in maintaining a unified ideology. For example, the colonization and defense role in the pre-state phase gave the kibbutz movement prestige and status. But does the kibbutz movement maintain this historic role in the present expansionist phase, when Jewish settlements in the occupied areas are a controversial and divisive national issue?

Second, how does the industrialization of the kibbutzim reconcile itself with its earlier land and farm oriented philosophy? The fact that its industrial output continues to be much less important to the overall economy than its agricultural production is bound to further reduce the significance of the kibbutz.[35] As one commentator has put it: there are signs of the kibbutzim becoming enclaves of rural collectivism with increasing irrelevance to their surroundings.[36] One would think that the Zionist mission of the kibbutz could have been put aside once the state was created and the emphasis could be placed on socialism but in fact the reverse has happened.

In spite of these difficulties it is obvious that the kibbutz is a successful model of an agro-industrial co-operative community unmatched in the capitalist world. It is a powerful example of the indigenous socialist tradition with its strong links to nationalism, its emphasis on community, and its ability to compete in a capitalist economy. Of the communist collectives the Chinese commune comes closest to it in practice. The kibbutz has been adept at responding to new economic needs and this has kept it alive, but the industrialization to which it has turned so successfully may end up undermining its unique character.

TANZANIA AND THE UJAMAA VILLAGE

Tanzania is a nation of fifteen million people on the East coast of Africa. It gained independence peacefully in 1961. There was no revolutionary war of liberation. In the twenty-five years since independence no other African state has been identified as much with co-operative group farming and the concept of socialist villages than has Tanzania.

In 1962, a few months after independence, the chairman of the ruling party, Julius K. Nyerere, issued a document called *Ujamaa-The Basis of African Socialism*, which described the ideology of the new state. The Swahili word 'ujamaa' referred to traditional sharing practices, which Nyerere called a kind of socialism. He felt that through 'ujamaa' Tanzania would develop its own African socio-economic identity. A number of agricultural producer co-ops were set up by party activists after this document was published and these projects became an inspiration for Nyerere to expand on his concept a few years later in a document called *The Arusha Declaration*, which was adopted as official party and government policy in 1967.

In the declaration Nyerere spoke of Tanzanian socialism as neither Marxist nor social democratic, but as a set of principles and practices rooted in the traditional patterns of production and exchange in pre-colonial Africa. He defined ujamaa socialism as meaning human equality and dignity; a society without exploitation of those who worked in it; and a system in which the means of production and exchange were firmly under the control of the people.[37] He was clearly opposed to importing any ideology from abroad and he believed fervently in the socialist nature of traditional African cultures. He spoke both as an African nationalist and an African socialist.

The Arusha Declaration stated that "the government actively assists in the founding and maintenance of co-operative organizations."[38] The focus of economic development was to be agricultural organizations set up by groups of people living and working in a community. These were called ujamaa (socialist) villages. Through ujamaa in the countryside, Tanzania would become self-reliant. Nyerere felt that persuasion rather than force would be the only element needed for success, but that is not what transpired.

In the 1960s 94 percent of Tanzania's population was agricultural and rural.[39] In terms of pure agrarianism, this percentage was greater than that of China's rural population in 1949 and Russia's in 1917. The Tanzanaians lived in very small, scattered, family-grouped settlements. They had a subsistence economy and a per capita income in 1967 of $150.[40] After independence the country had two elites: the Asians who controlled commerce and the educated urban blacks who controlled politics. In the first five years after the Arusha Declaration only 15 percent of the rural population joined Ujamaa villages.[41]

Why was the response so limited? First of all, it was a government idea yet voluntary. It came from above rather than from popular demand, yet it was not imposed. Second, there were no major economic benefits for the participants. As one writer has stated:

> Putting 30 people together to work with the old implements on 75 communal hectares instead of each working his own does not seem to bring any technical advantage to the producers.[42]

The same writer indicates that all that remained in Tanzania of traditional ujamaa practices after decades of colonialism was co-operation among family households. Private farming was the norm and grouping unrelated people together and expecting them to be instant practicioners of mutual aid was unrealistic. Nyerere was trying to build a future by returning to a past that had already disappeared. This meant the villagers did not know what was expected because the concept was unclear. The result was conflict between the government officials sent down to implement ujamaa and the peasants. In the villages themselves most of the land remained privately cultivated and only a small part was communal production. On top of this confusion were added bad management and bureaucratic excesses.

Because the ujamaa village concept was not being adopted fast enough, the government decided to force matters after 1973. Between 1973 and 1976 another 75 percent of the rural population was enrolled into villages, making a total of 90 percent of the rural population. By 1976, 13.5 million peasants were living in 7,300 villages.[43] The speed and completeness of the process is comparable to collectivization in Russia and China. But not all these villages were yet fully 'ujamaa,' i.e. multipurpose co-operative societies. The people were herded into them unwillingly. The civil service had decided that the minimum size of one of these villages should be 1,000, a large number in which to develop spontaneous feelings of co-operation and communal sharing.

Most observers agree that ujamaa villages have been a failure. Not only have they not improved the internal standard of living, but they have done nothing to decrease dependence on foreign aid and the international marketplace that regulates Tanzania's agricultural production. With the encouragement of the World Bank, Tanzania has substituted export cash crop production for traditional subsistance crops. Tea, tobacco, cotton, sugar and cashews are the primary exports. Now Tanzania has to import food to feed its people.[44] One can argue that it has been less than twenty years since the Ujamaa program was started—hardly long enough to evaluate such a major change. Nevertheless, to date the benefit to the population seems to be almost as unimpressive as that of the kolkhoz.

Marxist critics claim the whole ujamaa village idea is a throwback to utopian socialism and agrarian populism.[45] They criticize ujamaa as socialism based on idealistic morality rather than the reality of class struggle. Ujamaa did not make distinctions between classes among blacks since it was caught up in a broad anticolonial struggle of blacks versus whites. This lack of class analysis has hindered the proper, i.e. Marxist, implementation of socialism. Of the Marxist critics, Isaac G. Shivji thinks that ujamaa was basically an attempt to undermine the power of the Asian traders, which would indicate that there was class analysis but only for non-Blacks.[46] M. von Freyhold places the problem at the doorstep of poor planning, inadequate party leadership, and a vaguely defined view of communalism.[47] Others blame the wealthier peasants for sabotaging the system and the party functionaries for gross mismanagement.

The fact is that the policy was not popular among the peasantry and that the incentives were insufficient to attract people voluntarily. Forcing Ujamaa onto people only compounded the problems and heightened negative reaction. It is evident from our earlier examination of state-initiated collectives that these require a firm and unequivocal drive toward a specific social structure. The state establishes a system into which these organizations are bound and without which they cannot operate. This 'economic sense' was never established in Tanzania, where one had the shell of collectivity but not its substance. Ujamaa villages incorporated traditional communal practices with liberal democratic co-operatives ones and also maintained a commitment to private initiative. In short, the ujamaa villages exist in an ideological hodge-podge.

Likewise the voluntary approach was never given sufficent time to establish itself as a successful model as was the kibbutz. Since Ujamaa was based on an appeal to a utopian brand of African socalism, it is clear that only ideologically motivated people would respond. And in Tanzania these were a tiny minority. Of couse, this was insufficient for the government. It had a theory of African socialism, which it claimed was innate in the people's consciousness. If the people didn't respond its theory would have been unsubstantiated. No doubt Nyerere's motivation was sincere and his desire for an African road to socialism reflected the hopes of the time, but it proved to be ill-conceived. It lacked the strong arm of Marxist revolutions and a centrally planned economy that make communist collectives work; it lacked the utopian idealism and minority status that allows nongovernmental movements like the kibbutz to flourish; and it lacked a developed capitalist structure in which social democratic co-operative institutions test themselves and provide services.

Tanzania remained in the orbit of the international capitalist economy, which worked against its own socialist goals, and yet the state was too dictatorial to make ujamaa a voluntary grassroots movement. It was a confused and contradictory effort whose major result has been to weaken the validity of an indigenous African socialism.

SPAIN AND THE MONDRAGON CO-OPERATIVES

Compared to the troubled ujamaa villages of Tanzania, the Mondragon co-operatives in the Basque provinces of Spain are a model of success. Like Israel, Spain is a capitalist country and like Israel, it contains a good example of a flourishing community based on socialist and co-operative principles.

Mondragon is the name of a town of 30,000 people in the centre of the Basque country in northern Spain. Here, over the past twenty-five years there has developed a network of worker co-ops that has attracted global attention. Mondragon is the birthplace and focal point of over 100 co-ops that employee 19,000 worker-owners and provide education, housing, social welfare, consumer goods, and banking for its members. The first co-operative was launched in the late 1950s but the roots of the

Mondragon achievement reach back into the Spanish Civil War (1936-1939) and the co-operatively oriented teaching of the Catholic Church that developed at the turn of the century.

During the war between the right-wing insurgents led by General Franco and the left-wing supporters of the Republic revolutionary forms of industrial and rural organization mushroomed. In Catalonia, next to the Basque region, there was a powerful anarcho-syndicalist federation of unions called the CNT (Confederation Nacional del Trabajo), which encouraged and created worker-managed factories. The syndicalists, some one million strong in the summer of 1936, readily took over the means of production and showed that they were capable of running factories.[48]

Initially there was a spontaneous collectivization of both land and factories. Augustin Souchy described this movement involving hundreds of thousands of people as collectivization by the people themselves.[49] In Barcelona industries from railways to textiles were taken over by the workers. Daniel Guerin described how in October 1936 a congress representing 600,000 workers called for the socialization of industry.[50] One result was state recongnition of the socialized sector. But within a year the decree was suspended.[51]

In the rural areas the peasants took over the holdings of large landowners and pooled their production. In some areas even money was abolished. But the collectives were short-lived. The main reason was that the Republic itself lasted only three years before falling to Franco. As more and more territory was taken over by the Right less and less of the land and population was left in collectives. Besides, internal dissension and outright warring between the communists and anarchists on the Republican side undermined the collectives, which meant they were beseiged by the former internally as well as externally by Franco. Nevertheless, the social revolution that was waged in Republican Spain during the war effected many of the survivors and its radicalism was not lost.

The link between the civil war period and progressive catholicism came in the person of a young priest named Don Jose Maria Arizmendiarrieta, who had served in the Basque militia against Franco. After the war he was sent to the village of Mondragon as the parish priest. He was imbued with progressive Catholic social teaching on the dignity of work and the right of workers to participate in decision-making. His first achievement was a community-financed technical school for the children of workers. The five men who established the first industrial co-op at Mondragon were graduates of this school Arizmendi acted as the mentor of the co-op movement that evolved at Mondragon. His mixture of Christian socialism, Basque nationalism, and co-operative values was right for Mondragon.

With Arizmendi's prompting, the first co-operative was incorporated in 1958 as was the Caja Laboral Popular—the Working Peoples' Bank. It was a savings bank in which co-operatives and its own workers were owners. The Caja became the basic vehicle for financing many co-operative ventures associated with Mondragon. Within ten years there were over thirty co-ops affiliated and they employed 3,500 workers.[52] Most of the co-ops were in the metalwork and furniture business. Some were conversions from bankrupt capitalist firms and others were started from scratch.

Today the Mondragon system includes housing, educational, consumer and social welfare co-ops, but at its core is the system of worker co-ops, which are of two kinds: first-degree and second-degree. The first degree co-ops are production co-ops whose general assembly is composed solely of the workers employed in that co-op. The second-degree co-ops are those that service the first degree co-ops and have democratic control spread among several constituencies: their own employees and representatives of the primary co-ops. Of the co-ops in the Mondragon system, the great majority are first degree. In the case of the co-operative schools at Mondragon, voting is divided one-third co-ops, one-third employees, and one-third parents. In every case there is a serious commitment to democratic control by those who participate in the co-op.

Joining a Mondragon co-op requires that the new member purchase capital shares, some of which become collective property and the rest become his capital account to which is added his annual share of the co-op's profits. When the worker leaves the co-op, the value of his captial account is returned to him. At present it costs about $6,000 to become a worker-owner and this amount can be borrowed from the Caja but the two-year repayment period makes it a substantial investment, when annual salaries are approximately $10,000.

Mondragon has developed its own form of operation and principles of distribution of funds that ensure the survival of the co-op and its expansion. The supreme authority in the co-op is the general assembly of the workers, each of whom has one vote. The general assembly meets annually. For interim management there is an elected board that oversees operations and members are not paid for their management work. At Mondragon there is no hired labour except for a few specialists on contract. Besides the managing board there is a social council elected by the workers that deals with shop floor issues and union-type concerns such as job rotation and classification. The co-ops are highly egalitarian because they do not allow the wage of the highest paid worker to be more than three times the lowest paid. So the chairman of the bank has a salary of only three times that of a young worker starting out. In spite of this one observer has noted that the senior bank staff maintain a patrician attitude toward worker-members.[53]

The profits of the co-op are distributed in fixed proportions. Ten percent is allocated to social and educational projects in the community. This is a requirement of Spanish law in exchange for favourable tax status for co-ops. Twenty percent is given over to the collective reserves of the co-op and seventy percent is distributed to the individual capital share accounts of each worker in the co-op in proportion to his salary. Since few workers leave Mondragon this money is available for investment rather than being paid out in bonuses. The end result is that 90 percent of the surplus is made available to the co-op for its use. In 1978 this meant that Mondragon, employing only 3 percent of the Basque workers in manufacturing, invested 77 percent of all monies invested in the region's manufacturing that year.[54]

Mondragon has developed an impressive structure that provides an integrated system. A child of a Mondragon worker can attend a daycare co-operative, then go to a co-op Basque language elementary school, graduate to a technical high school, and attend the Mondragon engineering university. While at the university he can pay his way by working part-time at the student co-op factory. He can then get a job in a co-op, live in a Mondragon housing co-op, shop in the Eroski consumer co-op and on retirement get his pension from Lagun Aro, the social welfare co-op of Mondragon. During his tenure at Mondragon he is virtually guaranteed job security. Should his job become redundant he will be retrained and assigned to another co-op. In a region where unemployment runs 15 to 20 percent this is extremely important.

This extensive system of services has arisen partly from the fact that under Spanish law, worker-owners are considered self-employed and so do not benefit from the state social security measures. What has enabled this wide-ranging system to develop is the pivotal institution of the Caja. Under Spanish law, workers savings banks were allowed to pay 1 percent higher interest than commercial banks and this attracted the funds of many non-Mondragon Basques. The Caja provides two basic resources: financial and managerial. When a new enterprise is launched up to 70 percent of the capital comes from the Caja, 20 percent from the workers, and a further 10 percent from the state.[55] The bank does extensive feasibility studies and when it finally agrees to finance a new co-op, the co-op must sign a contract of association with the Caja that allows it to monitor its progress and step in if problems develop. This managerial assistance has been vital for the economic success of the co-ops, of which very few have failed.

Some critics have pointed a finger at the Caja as an infringement on self-management and they have criticized its all-powerful role.[56] There is no question that the Caja, with its managerial expertise, has created a dependency relationship. Mondragon is trying to deal with this issue by removing the managerial function to a new co-op and by creating a national assembly representing all the co-ops that would have ultimate control. In the new contract of association, the Caja would be only one of several supervising bodies at Mondragon.

Another issue that has arisen at Mondragon is the question of unions. Until 1977, independent unions were forbidden in Franco's Spain but since then they have become active and a dynamic element in the economy of the country. They have not penetrated Mondragon co-ops in any significant way because of the democratic worker-owner structure but they do pose an issue for the future. In 1974 Mondragon suffered its first and only economic strike. This was at the ULGOR plant, which employed several thousand workers. The leaders of the strike were fired and Mondragon has decided to limit production co-ops to less than 500 workers so that the misunderstandings that arise from large multi-tiered structures do not recur.

Besides the role of the Caja and the absence of unions, Mondragon has three other features. The first is its Basque orientation. All the co-ops are established only in the Basque-speaking region with many head-quartered in the town of Mondragon itself. The Mondragon co-ops are viewed as being committed to the economic and social development of the Basque people. Whenever a political strike is called by the major Basque parties, Mondragon responds with a sympathy shutdown. The second feature is its focus on industrial production. Seventy-five percent of the Mondragon co-ops are in the secondary industries, only five percent are in the primary sector (agriculture), and a further twenty percent are in the tertiary or service sector.[57]

With its core in the secondary industries, Mondragon has made industrial job creation and technological innovation its basic goals. Mondragon sees itself as creating employment for workers in the region and it ensures that it fulfills this mandate through judicious investment in the co-ops and the operation of a research and development institute (Ikerlan). The third feature that dovetails into this is Mondragon's unfailing emphasis on education. With its origins in a technical school for working class children, Mondragon has continued to expand its educational system so as to provide a steady stream of recruits for its enterprises. From daycare to university, Mondragon has one of the most extensive and integrated educational systems in Spain.

These factors have created a co-operative community at Mondragon, whose sophistication and influence is admired around the world. Some scholars consider Mondragon "a new phenomenon in co-operative history" which others attribute to "a highly coordinated system of co-operatives which has managed to remain economically viable while con-tributing to very broad goals of Basque development."[58] And like the kibbutz, it has not been replicated elsewhere in spite of efforts to draw on it for inspiration.[59] The reasons offered for Mondragon's success are usually multivaried. They range from the sensible requirement for a capital stake from every worker and the retention of that share until the worker leaves to the prudent management, excellent financing, and strong democratic character of the co-ops.[60] Strong leadership, co-operative philosophy, and the critical mass achieved by the Mondragon co-ops are also cited as strengths.

My own assessment of Mondragon is that its success is based on an uncanny ability to be both radical and conservative simultaneously. In this it refects the culture, society, and economy of the Basque region. The co-ops were tolerated by Franco's regime because they were economic and not political manifestations and were marginal and local in power. They did not pose a threat to the state. In their industrial focus they were simply reflecting the class composition of the population, of which 50 percent is industrial working class.[61] Mondragon grew out of the region and identified with the mainstream aspirations of the people. This basic connection with the wider society is crucial to the survival of any socialist community in a nonsocialist environment.

Although Mondragon does not have the communal features of the kib-butz, it has identified itself with the aspirations of the Basque people as fully as the kibbtuzim have identified with Israel. Yet the co-operative community at Mondragon is quite different because it reflects the in-digneous social limits of Basque culture. Its industrial commitment is as strong as that of the kibbutz to the land. Both Mondragon and the kib-butz have shown a great capacity to adapt to capitalist competition. They both have an excellent record of investment, which shows a willingness to defer immediate rewards in order to assure future returns.

Yet above all else it is the rootedness—their indigenous quality—that makes them outstanding. They are integral parts of their respective societies. Equally vital to success has been their minority status, which has protected them from destruction by capitalism, which does not view them as a serious threat. Yet their small numbers have been sufficiently large to capture the imagination and acceptance of their fellow citizens. They are viewed as an economic and social vanguard for national aspira-tions rather than socialism. This has allowed the kibbutz to establish a socialist standard for agricultural communities and for Mondragon to create a model of a system of worker co-operative socialism.

WORKER CO-OPS IN THE U.K., THE U.S., AND CANADA

The United Kingdom, the United States, and Canada are three English-speaking countries with worker co-operatives. In these countries, the liberal democratic form of co-operative is prevalent and this has moved worker co-ops in that direction rather than along socialist lines. Basically they emphasize the Rochdale rules, single function co-ops, and private property.

Each of these countries has witnessed a rebirth in worker ownership that reflects its only national tradition. In Great Britain high unemployment resulting from Conservative government policies has created a wave of small worker co-ops promoted and funded by local municipal town councils, which can be found in every part of the United Kingdon and they operate on co-operative principles of one person/one vote.[62] Under the leadership of groups such as the Industrial Common Ownership Movement and the Scott-Bader Commonwealth they have come to represent an increasingly popular alternative to unemployment. Although worker co-ops are only grudgingly accepted by Britain's powerful trade unions and by the country's resurgent business interests, they have won some small degree of approval from each of the political parties. However they lack a substantial endorsement. In short, at the national political level they are tolerated, but not much more. This has allowed them to proliferate but not overcome the major problems of long-term viability that a significant government program could address.

Jenny Thornley says that British worker co-ops suffer from a "fundamentally weak capital structure."[63] There is simply nothing like Mondragon's Caja Laboral Popular. She also points out that they are not connected to the powerful consumer co-op establishment in Great Britain. They are basically scattered around the country, not integrated with each other, possess no focal point and lack a united development strategy, though some federating efforts are emerging. The attempt by the Wales Trade Union Council to create a Mondragon model has not succeeded because of divided opinions in the trade union movement, the coal-mining base of the region's economy, and the underdevelopment of Welsh nationalism compared to Basque nationalism.

In Britain the worker co-op idea does not have a sufficient institutional consensus behind it nor a large enough economic mass to pull together its piecemeal development. There is little in its present evolution that would suggest a movement toward a socialist co-operative community structure like Mondragon's or Israel's kibbutzim. Because of trade union and business opposition the movement is limited to a variety of small individual enterprises. Because of a long tradition of Labour Party nationalization, any large factories would most likely end up being nationalized rather than socialized.

While the British model retains a strong co-operative core, the Americans have not even gone as far as the Rochdale model for their worker ownership. Since the mid-Seventies, the most common route for worker ownership has been the Employee Share Ownership Plan (ESOP) through which employees have purchased shares in their firms. Under the American model, voting power is dependent on the number of shares one owns. For example, in the employee-owned firm of Republic Hose Manufacturing in Youngstown, Ohio, 52 percent of the firm is held by management personnel and there are no workers on the board of directors.[64]

The ESOP approach has been used in buyouts by workers of large plants that are about to be shutdown. A typcial example is that of the 5,500 workers of a steel mill in West Virginia who have purchased their plant for $181 million. Their union has agreed to reduce labour costs by 32 percent to make the plant competitive and the workers have agreed to having a majority of the board of directors come from outside the firm to make it acceptable to the banks.[65]. One researcher on worker buyouts estimates that sixty companies were bought out between 1980 and 1982 when they were threatened with closure. (In 1982 619 plants closed down with a loss of 215,500 jobs) She says that these buyouts saved 50,000 jobs.[66] This is a significant development in which whole towns have been saved from death.

The problem with the share-ownership model is that the firm can easily revert to private ownership. In one case a local entrepreneur offered a worker-owned mine $1,834 for each share that had been originally bought for $50 and he won control of the company. The miners agreed to sell when the banks refused to loan them funds for the mine's expansion, but the banks had no such problem when it was privatized.[67] This indicates that ESOPs may actually facilitate the saving of private firms through an interim step which merely prepares it for private ownership later on.

In a cover story titled "Revolution or ripoff?" *Business Week* magazine questioned the meaning of ESOPs. Predicting that 25 percent of the American workforce will own part or all of their firms by the the year 2000, the article shows that ESOPs are being used by management to prevent unwanted takeovers, to open up pension funds, and to reduce wages and control unions.[68]

It is clear that employee ownership has provided an effective option to plant shutdown, but it is being done in a nonco-operative way. Share-ownership perpetuates a capitalist share structure and a temptation for workers to sellout when they have made the firm successful once more.

Yet the ESOP is not the only model of employee ownership in the U.S. though it is the most recent and the most popular.

After the First World War a plywood mill was built by workers on the West coast of the U.S. and organized along true worker co-op lines. Today, one-eighth of the plywood made in the United States is produced by such co-ops. They range in size from 80 to 450 workers and gross from $3 to $15 million annually.[69] The record shows that these co-ops do not lay off workers during a slump and that they consistently make more profit than private firms in spite of being egalitarian in their salary structure.

Their success and longevity is based on their being part of a single industry; their grouping in a single geographic area; and the low capital requirements to start a plant. In many ways they are classic producer co-ops. But as a model for worker co-operatives they have not spawned similar projects in other sectors. Perhaps it is the European co-operative background of the immigrants who created these co-ops that has been their secret of success and also a limit on their appeal.

Today's ESOPs have been sold by business as a way to involve more workers with capitalist practices since only 6 percent of Americans own 80 percent of all shares.[70] ESOPs are viewed as a kind of fringe benefit, like profit-sharing, without any socialist content. They do not foster industrial democracy, nor do they encourage worker self-management. Instead they are viewed as another way of increasing private income. Since neither nationalization of large plants nor of an entire industry is practised in the U.S., ESOPs have become the only ideologically acceptable way of saving jobs and communities. It is interesting to note that ESOPs are thriving in the dying industrial areas but are not popular in the new growth industries and areas.

Canada has neither the small community-based worker co-ops of the U.K. nor the ESOPs of the large unionized plants of the U.S. It has only just begun to move toward worker co-ops. At present there are about 200 worker co-ops in Canada.[72] The Province of Quebec leads the way in this field, especially in its forestry sector.[73] But the movement is too young to have a definite character as yet.

The direction in which worker co-ops will go in Canada will be a reflection of the country's political economy. Since it is central Canada that is most industrialized, it is likely that any significant worker co-op movement will occur there. And since foreign ownership is a major factor in Canadian industry and so much production is carried on by subsidiaries of foreign (mostly American) firms, it is most likely that worker co-ops will be forced to develop in either the Canadian-owned small business sector or the state-owned crown corporations. With Canada's long history of state involvement in economic development, there will likely be some degree of state involvement in a national progarm. As well, the national co-operative movement will have input into worker co-ops which is not the case in either the U.S. or Great Britain. The National Task Force on Co-operative Development, sponsored by the established co-op system, stated that "the development of worker co-operatives in Canada is a stable, democratically based source of Canadian employment and economic development."[74] It would seem that the small business sector worker co-ops will end up like contemporary British worker co-ops, while the large crown corporations that the new Conservative government will try to privatize may very well end up as ESOP-type institutions.

At present the handful of non-Quebec worker co-ops in Canada are very small. Their roots are in the Sixties and Seventies counter culture. But with a projected national unemployment rate of over 10 percent for the rest of the decade and a new Conservative federal government with ideological links to the economic politics of the U.K. and the U.S., the stage is set for worker co-ops in Canada, if for no other reason than the growth of employee ownership in Canada's sister economies.

Worker co-ops in Canada will follow the liberal democratic pattern of co-operatives that is dominant in the country. As a late-comer to worker co-ops Canada will be able to draw on other national experiences to which it is politically and economically related. For example, the British trade union movement has been a major proponent of nationalization and so it has found worker co-ops hard to accept, but the U.S. trade union movement has not been threatend by the ESOPs because their capitalist-like management leaves the union's role very much intact and continues their tradition of business unionism. Canada will most likely end up with a dual system of worker co-ops in the small business sector and E.S.O.P.s in the plants that employ hundreds and thousands of workers. There is little likelihood of anything approaching Mondragon.

THE IDEOLOGY OF SOCIALIST CO-OPERATIVE COMMUNITIES

Socialist co-ops have developed a successful balance between their internal socialist operating principles and the external capitalist reality in which they must compete. The only system that has not developed such a balance is the government-created ujamaa villages. This would indicate that socialist communities need voluntary citizen participation to work effectively.

This ideological adrenalin flows from two sources: socialism and nationalism. These are the idealistic loyalties that propel people to create or join socialist co-ops and they are as important a motivator as practical

concerns. The difficulty is that this high degree of ideological commitment results in a socialist internal structure externalized into the wider
society. Socialist ideologues who are not prepared to work for a total
socialist state, the way Marxists are, opt for an immediate mini-society.
They create exemplary models of socialist life and production. And exemplary models tend to attract only a tiny minority. Their focus on purity and strictness is enhanced by the small community structure which
does not have to compromise its internal principles with the larger society
unless forced to do so by the state. It would seem that socialist co-ops
need a nonsocialist context in order to thrive.

The strategy of proliferating socialist communities under capitalism as
a way of creating an egalitarian society, of which socialist co-ops tend
to speak, has not worked because the energy required to maintain ideals
internally leaves little for external work. The only national consensus that
exists is nationalistic and nonsocialist. Since socialist co-ops depend on
this nonsocialist nationalism and identify with it, they end up promoting
a nonsocialist reality in the country as a whole. So far, Mondragon has
not had to face this problem because Basque nationalism has not achieved sovereignty, but, if it should, then Mondragon would face the same
pressures as the kibbutz.

Nationalism has also affected the transferability of exemplary models
to other countries. The indigenous national roots that give socialist co-
ops so much power, also result in their being rather narrow in appeal
since they are a response to a particular environment. One would think
that socialism was a universal value, but since in the case of socialist co-
ops it is married to nationalism, that socialism becomes particular and
localized in its practices.

The socialist model has shown itself to be tuned to modernization.
Socialist communities have a good record of technological innovation.
Since they are forced to provide for a community through economic expansion they work hard to maintain a progressive industrial and
agricultural profile, often in advance of the general national standard in
either the private or public sectors. The other side of this technological
progressivism is the sacrifice expected of socialist community members.
Because they are often pioneering efforts which begin in poverty, they
operate in a puritanical spirit of hard work and self-sacrifice. The emphasis on the common good is so strong that commitment is to the welfare
of future generations rather than immediate gratification.

Socialist co-ops are also characterized by a lack of charismatic personalities in their leadership. Certainly Gordon, Arizmendi, and Nyerere
played the role of ideological father-figure, but they did not create communities around themselves. They were collectively developed with

many loci of power. The communities did not owe allegiance to the guiding genius of a single guru, but to an idea.

The ideology of socialist co-operatives reconciles socialism and nationalism by creating socialist communities that have a national non-socialist development purpose. The vehicle of small communities created a series of exemplary models which were unable to attract more than a tiny minority within the nation or to replicate themselves in other countries or regions. They create a revolution for themselves and not for others. Because they are tied to pluralistic states and their interest in the state is more nationalistic than socialistic they have ended up providing a high degree of socialism for the few. And where they have tried to create socialism for the many, as in Tanzania, they have failed. In some profound sense, socialist co-ops have shown themselves to be an individual rather than a public answer to capitalism.

Chapter Five:
THE COMMUNALIST TRADITION

A DEFINITION

The word 'communalist' refers to that co-operative tradition which has also been called 'utopian,' 'intentional,' and 'communitarian.' It refers to those voluntary, small-scale communities in which co-operation is all-encompassing and in which egalitarian values and practices, group ownership and control are supreme. One author has summarized the communalist tradition as "a record of the individuals and groups who have attempted to live communally, sharing material goods and a common lifestyle."[1]

If the liberal democratic tradition may be considered as the rightwing of co-operation, then communalism may be designated its leftwing because communalists are highly restricted in the amount and kind of private property that they may possess. All land, earned income, and community goods are owned and distributed by a corporate entity.[2] Although Marxist collectives and socialist communities are also on the leftwing of co-operation and share features with communalism, their communism is not as intense as that found in most examples of communalism. Even in the case of the kibbutz, there are major differences with the communalism to be examined in this chapter.

Four features distinguish communalism from the other traditions. First, communalism is fundamentally isolationist in orientation. The separatist impulse to withdraw from society and set oneself apart is rooted in the belief that the commune's distinct values can be preserved only be leaving society. Because the communalist impluse seeks "more intense and closely knit communities" and "a pattern of existence which is [its] own creation" it forges an internal universe of its own, where the members attempt to live together in "harmony, brotherhood, and peace."[3]

This instinct to withdraw is often rooted in a fervent social or religious criticism and a strong rejection of current mores. In some cases the withdrawal is complete, while in other cases it is only a temporary step prior to proselytization. This anti-societal and inward orientation is not found the other traditions.

The second feature of communalism is its origins in charismatic leadership. Communes are founder-based and founder-oriented. At the origin of each communal movement one finds a strong personality. For monasticism it was St. Benedict, for early nineteenth century utopian communities it was Robert Owen, and for the Hutterites it was the Anabaptist martyr Jacob Huter, all of whom built a community around themselves. The practice of naming communal movements after their founders is a way of distinguishing communes from other co-ops.

Communal dependence on a dominant personality is expressed not only in reverence for the founder, but also in the social structure of the commune. They are clearly hierarchical, though the leadership is elected and goods are equally shared. Often the highest office in the commune is for life. And one can even distinguish successful from failed communes by dividing them into those that survive the lifespan of the founder and those that do not. As one scholar of nineteenth century Owenite colonies stated bluntly:

> Owenism was essentially a sect which emerged round a leader whose teaching was accepted by followers, and which did not institutionally survive his death.[4]

Charimastic leadership creates a follower syndrome among members. This is not the case in the other co-op traditions, which generally emphasize self-initiative. The charismatic leader issues a call to achieve a higher degree of human perfection. This places high standards of performance on the members and results in a kind of superior or elite mentality among communalists. When one combines charismatic leadership with the commune's physical and psychic separation from society, one finds they tend to operate as mini-societies, whose primary wish is noninterference by the wider society in which they are situated.

The end result of the isolationist and leadership characteristics is communalism's third feature: small, intimate community structure.

Communes are much smaller than either the socialist communities or Marxist collectives to which they are related. It is not just the strict standards to which communalists adhere that limits their appeal and therefore their size; it is their ideology as well. It emphasizes face to face relations. Charles Erasmus insists that the ''reciprocal altruism'' that communalism demands is most potent in groups of up to 100 members.[5] In the small community in which everyone knows the others the bonding required to withstand external pressures is more easily achieved.[6] "Communal life" writes Rosabeth Kanter, "depends on a continual flow of energy and support among members, on their depth of shared relationship, and on their continued attachment to each other and to the joint endeavour."[7]

As a small grouping without much external support, communes are very aware of the importance of interpersonal relations within the group and how personal activities must be channeled and monitored for the good of the community. Since communes are voluntary organizations based on idiosyncratic values, they cannot depend on public pressure or civil authority to ensure compliance among members. Instead, the commune must exert the kind of pressure used by families and other intimate groups.

The fourth feature of communalism is its total egalitarianism in ownership, production, and consumption, all of which aims to eliminate economic or material disparity. These values exist in both streams of communalism: the religious and the political. In the religious tradition, this egalitarianism is rooted in religious teachings of how mankind ought to comport itself in regard to others; in the political tradition it is rooted in secular socialist and communist values of equal sharing. A major study of Hutterites points out that communal life "is believed to be the divine order of God, who from the beginning created all things for common use," and that "every member shall give and devote all his or her time, labour, services, earnings and energies to...the community."[8] Private possessions and privacy are limited in exchange for which the community ensures equal distribution of communal goods.

The characteristics of egalitarianism, intimate community structure, charismatic leadership, and isolationism bind communes into a single tradition, but their idiosyncratic roots in different leaders and in various philosophies and values means they do not relate well to each other. There is little perceived commonality by the members of a Hutterite colony, of a monastery, or of a counterculture commune. Since their beliefs are different, even when their practice is similar, their common communal lifestyle is insufficient to overcome differences. Communes that survive do so by clinging tenaciously to their own particular ideology.

In examining the communalist tradition we will be looking at both the religious and secular streams and their manifestations in Western Canada. Under the religious category we will be dealing with Christian monasticism, the Hutterite sect, and the Doukhobours, as well as nineteenth century American utopian communities of various kinds.

Under the political category we will examine the work of the utopian socialists of the nineteenth century in both Britain and the U.S., the counterculture communes of the U.S. that began in the 1960s, as well as several indigenous regional examples of communalism.

Because of the great variety of communal life over the centuries, communes are often identified by how they differ from each other rather than by what they share, but these differences are simply the varied flowering of a common utopian impluse to create a more perfect society on earth. The factors that have helped some of these experiments to survive and forced others to disappear are as numerous as the communes themselves. Survival for inward-looking communities has never been easy, but their constant reappearance throughout history indicates that they are a basic thrust of the human spirit.

THE RELIGIOUS STREAM

The religion of occidental communalism is Christianity. It is divided into two traditions: Catholic and Protestant. The Catholic communal tradition is priestly monasticism, while the Protestant communal tradition is the utopian community of believers. The founder of monasticism was the sixth century Roman, St.Benedict, who established the religious 'rule' (comparable to the objects and bylaws of a corporation) which emphasized a community of monks as opposed to the earlier Byzantine tradition of the solitary anchorite. Besides this community aspect, the Benedictine rule encouraged the monks to be self-supporting rather than live on charity.[9]

Benedictine monasticism rose to great power and influence in the medieval period, when monasteries were not only widespread but also centres of intellectual and economic life. The Benedictines cleared farmland, encouraged handicrafts and peasant agriculture, and became both religious and secular authorities within feudal society. Of course, corruption accompanied this power and wealth. Charles Erasmus points out that "the history of monasticism after Benedict is a history of reform movements each trying to reassert the original Benedictine rules of austerity and organization."[10]

The monk voluntarily renounced the life of the world when he joined the community and professed the vows of poverty, chastity, and obedience. The vow of poverty meant the surrender of private property, both past and future, and the sharing of the monastery's "community of goods." Following the New Testament injunction "If thou wouldst be perfect, go, sell what thou hast and give to the poor, and come, follow me" the monk was asked to emulate the life of Christ and the early

Christian communities. The following reference in the Acts of the Apostles is often cited as authority for communal Christian life:

> And all that believe were together, and held all things in common; and sold their possessions and goods, and parted them to all men, as every man had need. (Acts 2:44-4)

The vow of Christian poverty meant that the monk had to place all that he had at the disposal of the monastic community, to receive the support of the community in exchange, and to share in the responsibility for the material life of the community.[11] In a contemporary monastic community, this means that the income earned from teaching, pastoral work, farming and other enterprises becomes the property of the monastic community and the monk is given shelter, clothing, food, and travel allowances as approved by the monastic authorities.

But it would be wrong to think that monastic life is centred primarily on the community of goods. It relies more on the community of spiritual life—the religious ritual—that makes up a day. As one monk explained, "the concept of a religious community is dearer than the concept of a community of goods."[12] Monasticism means the complete sharing of a total way of life. The common religious practices bind the members through daily contact, shared ideals, the very project of monasticism itself in which they are separated from society, and the deep-rooted traditions of their fraternity and community.

The contemporary liberation theologian Alejandro Cussianovich states that the monastic tradition "has frequently presented the life of the monk as a continuation of the life of the early Christian community" because of its emphasis on sharing.[13] Although he feels that monastic-like Christian communities can be created among Catholic lay people without the three vows, it is clear that historically Catholic communalism expressed itself primarily through the priestly monastic ideal.

Monasticism is a way of life in which personal attributes such as unselfishness, joyfulness, and calmness are vital to the cohesion of the community.[14] These personal values are encouraged through a rite of passage in which one leaves behind a ordinary world and enters a new environment. Those wishing to enter a monastery serve a lengthy apprenticeship as novices prior to taking their final vows. This rite of passage, which may involve ordination to the priesthood, makes it clear "to both the person involved and everyone in the community that the structure of their social world has changed."[15]

The monastic tradition has spread beyond the monastery itself into most religious orders in Catholicism, where the three vows are now the basic norm. Thus the community of goods is practised in a variety of nonmonastic religious orders, both male and female. This means that tens of thousands of members of religious orders today practice some form of communal lifestyle, even if they do not live in a formal monastery.

Monasticism provides an excellent example of the four features of communalism. First it involves a flight from the world, even though monastic activities have often contributed to its material wealth. Second, it originated in charismatic personalities, many of whom became saints. Thirdly, it encouraged a small size. Even though in the medieval period some monasteries were huge complexes controlling a number of villages and their peasant workers, the general rule was the establishment of a new monastery when one got too large. These new monasteries tended to govern themselves independently of other monasteries. Fourthly, monasticism has been strict in its adherence to the ideal of a community of goods if not to the vow of poverty itself. However the principles applied only to members, who formed a spiritual elite.

Historically, the ethos of the monastery has been familial in tone and agrarian in occupation and this has continued to the present day in that contemporary monasteries in Europe and North America are found in rural areas, where farming is of prime importance. As a form of community life the monastery offers the monk "a high degree of personal intimacy, emotional depth, moral commitment, social cohesion, and continuity in time."[16] It also offers him status.

As an institution that is fifteen centuries old, monasticism is one of the great examples of successful communalism. Although monasteries today are only very pale reflections of their medieval importance, they continue to exist and to serve as a model of both a successful community of goods and a successful community of the spirit.

In contrast to the Catholic tradition is the Protestant utopian community of true believers. It is nonpriestly and nonmonastic and encompasses men, women, and children. Two prominent examples of this tradition—the Hutterites and the Doukhobours—will be discussed later in this chapter in the section on Western Canada. First we will examine nineteenth century Chrisian communal sects in the United States. Rosabeth Kanter, an authority on American communalism, describes the United States as the site "for the founding of hundreds—perhaps thousands—of utopian communities, from religious sects that retreated to the wilderness as early as 1680 to the vast number of communes today [1972]."[17]

The frontier of the United States, which was continually being pushed further West by progressive settlement, offered the opportunity for those who wished to establish their own communities far from society. In the Protestant Christian tradition, in which the priesthood of all believers and individual divine inspiration is accepted, it is not unusual for new Christian sects to be generated by those who were unhappy with their Christian life.

All the successful nineteenth century religious communes in the U.S. began as some kind of Christain group.[18] These included the Oneida Perfectionists, the Shaker Believers, the Amana Inspirationists, and the Rappites. The Shakers began in the late eighteenth century as a millenarian cult, that is, one which looked forward to the second coming of Christ. It lasted until the early twentieth century, even though it was a celibate movement that had to propagate itself through the adoption of orphans. At its peak in the mid-nineteenth century it had 6,000 adherents living in twenty villages.[19]

The Oneida community was set up by John Humphrey Noyes, who called his sect the Perfectionists. It was small in size—in 1874 it had 219 adults and 64 children—but it employed 270 workers.[20] Oneida practised 'complex marriage' and communal child-rearing. Public outrage at Noyes' sexual practices led to his fleeing the country and Oneida becoming a wealthy joint stock company in 1881. In religious communes such as Oneida, people lived in dormitory-style housing, ate communally, and created their own educational and social services as well as flourishing farms and small industries. The following Oneida song captures the communal spirit of the time:

> We have built us a dome
> On our beautiful plantation
> And we all have one home
> And one family relation [21]

The Rappites, named after their leader George Rapp, are a fairly typical example of this kind of communalism. Founded in 1805 by German religious dissenters who established three settlements, first at Harmony, Pennyslvannia; then Harmony, Indiana; and finally, Economy, Ohio, the Rappites had a peak population of 1,700.[22] When one signed the Articles of Association, one gave over all property to the society, pledged to submit to its rules, and to relinguish all claims to reimbursement on withdrawal.[23] Like other millenarian sects, Rappites practised celibacy. They established their own town, their own schools, a bank (Farmers Bank of Harmony), numerous local industries, and a very productive farming operation. They were visited and studied by the notables of the day.

In 1824, the Rappites sold Harmony, Indiana to Robert Owen and moved to Ohio. Eventually the lack of new German immigrants and the practice of celibacy took their toll. George Rapp died in 1847 and though the society continued formally till 1916 it went into decay with fewer and fewer members and most of its earnings coming from investments rather than productive labour. Their life is now remembered through the museums established at the sites of their settlements.

These nineteenth century religious communes exemplified the isolationism, charismatic leadership, limited size, and community of goods that characterize the communal tradition. Though they sometimes peaked at a large size, they were unable to sustain this population. If one averages their membership over their lifespan, it is usually small and village size. It was their religious faith that ensured compliance with communal norms and their communal work style that made them rich. But idiosyncratic values, such as celibacy, eventually caused their demise or dissolution into capitalist enterprises that kept the remaining and aging members in comfort. Even so these religious communes fared much better than their political counterparts.

THE POLITICAL STREAM

The leading example of secular or political communalism in the English-speaking world was the communities established by Robert Owen (1771-1858). One of Britain's most successful industrialists who became a prominent social reformer and philanthropist, Owen made "the first attempt of any significance to form a purely secular community."[24]

The main source of Owen's wealth was his ownership of the New Lanark Mills in Scotland, which he and several partners bought in 1799. It was the largest cotton spinning mill in the country, employing 1400-1500 workers, the majority of whom were women.[25] After Owen took over New Lanark, he turned it into a model factory, and a community that was unusual for its day. While retaining the capitalist structure of the enterprise, he made major advances in improving the lot of the workers. He reduced the hours of work to ten and a half per day, restricted child labour to those ten years of age and over, and provided cheap housing and schooling for a nominal fee. There was even a savings bank for workers and a store that sold goods at cost. It was paternalism at its best and it made a difference in the lives of workers:

> When he took it over, New Lánark was ridden with poverty, disease, prostitution, promiscuity, and alcoholism. The strict

discipline resulted in clean, vermin-free homes, co-operative enterprises, lectures, dances in the evening, social security and eventual prohibition of drink.[26]

In 1824, at the age of fifty-three, Owen left New Lanark to found a new community in America. He bought the town of Harmony from the Rappites for $125,000, renamed the place New Harmony, and proceeded to advertise for settlers. About a thousand people were eventually enrolled but the experiment failed. In 1829, Owen handed over the property to his children, and in exchange for a small annuity returned to Britain, where he became a leader of the emerging trade union and co-operative movements.

In Britain, Owen's name became associated with the new word "socialism" which appeared in the 1820s. It was a blend of "communitarian theory, anti-capitalist economics, and a science of society."[27] It was a socialism that promoted community effort and generally sought the abolition of private property, and an improvement in the economic and moral life of the working class. In his communalist days Owen had felt that all this would come about through enlightened government, but his communal failure in America and the rise of major working class organizations in Britain like the Chartists convinced him that mass action was the only way to go. Besides, he had no more money left for utopian dreams.

After Owen it would not be until the 1960s that politically inspired communalism would return to prominence. During the long hiatus the older communalism was overtaken by the popularity of liberal democratic co-ops in the latter part of the nineteenth century and by communist collectives in the twentieth. The failure of the early "utopian" communites gave Marx reason to attack this kind of socialism and to condemn it as unworkable while offering his own historical approach to class struggle. But Marx never completely rejected the communalist utopia; he placed it at the end of his historical vision—the creation of a communist world.

The reasons for the failure of political communalism in the nineteenth century are numerous. A lack of discrimination in selecting members, paternalistic ideology, and vague humanism contributed to its demise. The utopian community concept was based on an idealistic hope that others would copy the model. But the political economy of capitalism was evolving independently of communalism and pushing the masses in other directions.

Communalism criticized the industrial revolution for its social inequity but what it proved was that paternalism of the sort found at New

Lanark was compatible with capitalism but that the radical communalism of New Harmony was not. The pressure to conform, the demands of reconciling an internal system of socialism with a non-socialistic economy, and the limited appeal of its ideas meant that political communalism was viewed as impractical.

The next great surge of secular communalism burst on the historical stage in the 1960s and it was as short-lived as New Harmony. A contemporary photograph of a young man and woman with long hair standing in a field, she barefoot, he with a hoe in his hand, captures the spirit of the communal movemnt of the Sixties in the United States.[28] This was a mass movement made up of thousands of small group experiments that touched the lives of tens, if not hundreds, of thousands of young Americans. Compared to the nineteenth century experiments, the new communalism was a tidal wave—big, overwhelming, and short-lived.

This new communalism was part of a broad social phenomenon called the counterculture. Its general ethos was retreat from established norms through music, drugs and a return to the land where one would live naturally with limited technology. The politics of the counterculture were anti-war and ecological. Images of the counterculture ranged from teepees and geodesic domes to blue jeans and beads. As in all communalism, distinctiveness in dress and accomondation was encouraged. The larger society responded to the counterculture communes the way it did to previous communalism—with disapproval. The communalists were labelled "hippies."

The counterculture was a youth or student revolt universal in the industrialized nations and its answer to contemporary ills was the rural commune. This was especially true of the United States. The movement was a mix of religious and secular communalism with the religious communes lasting longer than the political ones. The religious communes were encouraged by cults that were in turn accused of brainwashing adherents. Various groupings have persisted into the 1980s.

The secular communes that arose at the same time were a reflection of the 'New Left' ideology, which was a blend of populism and anarchism, and the alternate lifestyle movement, which was both apolitical and nonreligious in the classic meaning of those words of not belonging to an organized political ideology or religious denomination. The secular movement was "deeply intertwined with the history of rural nostalgia" in the United States but the limited viability of such nostalgia meant the rapid demise of rural communalism.[29] One observer claims the number of rural communes peaked at 3,500 in 1970.[30] Most disappeared within a few years. What these communes lacked, writes

Rosabeth Kanter, is the "many strict and demanding social practices" of earlier nineteenth century communes.[31] In counterculture communes, the emphasis was on individual freedom expressed in the slogan "Do your own thing."

Added to the rural nostalgia was the theme of the extended family. The young were in revolt against the nuclear family, its isolated individualism and devotion to private property. They wanted equality and sharing. Since most were of middle-class, white origin these issues were real enough for them. But the young of the workers and the poor had no such bourgeois standard to rebel against. Since the communes attracted mostly young people, family structure was no more than a small grouping of peers. It did not represent a multi-generation reality.

Besides the themes of rural nostalgia and the extended family, the communalists emphasized personal intimacy, equality of children and adults, peace and love, and the creation of a world which would not participate in the 'military-industrial' complex of the larger society.[32] Although the communes were temporary they did bring to light the precariousness of the nuclear family and the need for support systems for adults and children beyond the traditional ones, as well as the ecological imbalance of urban society.[33] Even though the secular communes themselves were generally shortlived, they did provide an environment for the practice of these values, which were carried into the larger society with the communalists who returned. Through the communes passed a generation of social activists of one kind or another who upon leaving propagated their beliefs through more traditional channels. This positive result only highlighted the failure of secular communalism to make an impact in its own right as a strategy for social change. One had to leave a commune to foster social change.

In spite of their large number, the communes existed on the margins of American society because they were shortlived, almost faddish in nature, disapproved by the majority of citizens, and limited to the young of one class. The following rather harsh but realistic assessment of American communalism is echoed to some degree by a number of commentators:

> American communitarianism has always functioned as a deviant, radical, or otherworldly fringe, drawing off idealists, social malcontents, and dreamers rather than finding...a place for itself within the structure of societal institutions.[34]

But this author admits that communalism has become more accepted now than it was fifteen years ago and another writer claimed that 1,000 of the original 3,500 rural communes were still in operation in 1978.[35] How many of them have lasted into the mid-1980s and how many remain secular is uncertain.

In spite of the legacies of the counterculture such as the natural health food co-operative found in every major North American city and the remnants of rural communes, one must agree with Paul Starr, who in his essay ''The Phantom Community'' concluded that ''in the absence of general social transformation, counterinstitutions can survive only in certain limited forms.''[36] Those limited forms have ended up being either liberal democratic co-ops providing one specific service or religious cult communes.

The problem with these experiments is that they had no focal point. They were spontaneous, rapidly multiplying and rapidly disintegrating phenomena, which were closely tied to pop youth culture. New fads, new media values, new historical and socio-economic conditions affected them adversely as the pendulum swung to conservatism. In Canada, the communal movement was an American import, coming across the border with thousands of war resisters and the dominance of American culture in the media. The same clothing, lifestyle, and concerns were adopted in Canada and the life-cycle of the communes was basically the same as the American product. Though Canada did have a leftwing nationalist movement among its youth, communalism itself had no indigenous characteristics. A Canadian Council on Social Development report of 1974 described communal ideology as one of 'self-actualization' for the children of the middle class and the communal movement itself as one characterized by mobility and fluidity, i.e. transience.[37]

Contemporary secular communalism has had as poor a record as its nineteenth century counterpart. It has not created a stable model of communal life. Lacking the power of the state to enforce conformity as is common in communist countries, and lacking the strong ideological focus provided by socialism and nationalism in socialist communities, political communes have proven to be more ephemeral than their religious counterparts. Political communes have tended to express rebellion rather than revolution.

While the religious communes of this and the previous century used divine authority to maintain discipline and conformity and to guide lifestyle, the secular communes lacked an ideology to maintain people in isolated environments for long periods of time, while society itself remained antagonistic. That in the end is the contradiction of secular communalism—it seeks to escape society and simultaneously transform it. The religious communes have generally given up on 'this earthly realm' and so have let all their energies flow inward. Robert Owen learned long ago that ensuring escape from society and transforming it are mutually exclusive.

THE UTOPIAN TRADITION IN WESTERN CANADA

Communalism in Western Canada follows the basic division of this tradition into religious and secular-political manifestations. The most prominent of the religious communes are monasteries and settlements of Doukhobours and Hutterites. On the political side are several agricultural co-operative communities established at such places as Matador, Saskatchewan. As is generally the case, the religious communes in the region are more widespread and successful than the political ones.

The monastic tradition in this region is exemplified by St. Peter's Abbey, a Benedictine monastery at Muenster, Saskatchewan. Founded at the turn of the century when the area was being first settled by German-American colonists, the abbey was a transplant of a faltering monastery in the United States and was meant to provide pastoral care for new immigrants. The abbey has provided educational facilities for the youth of the area, including university-level instruction. It publishes a newspaper for the Catholics of Saskatchewan and Manitoba as well as being engaged in the traditional pursuits of farming and parish work. It is situated a good distance from the nearest city and its agrarian tradition encourages self-sufficiency.[38]

Even though the number of monks is steadily declining (59 in 1959 to 48 in 1984), it is still a sizeable monastery in the loose federation of seventeen 'houses' in North America to which it belongs. When a man joins the monastery, he ordinarily enters without any material assets. For the past 15 years the monastery has also required the signing of a contract which describes the legal limits of his claims on the community. The applicant is a 'novice' for one year and then can take temporary vows for three years, after which he can take final vows. With the final vows, the new monk signs a will donating his personal assets to the monastery. Should a monk leave the monastery permanently, he may receive a modest financial grant to help establish himself in the secular world.[39]

Tasks in the monastery are assigned and the vow of obedience encourages rotation of offices so that no one monk will try to make himself indispensable in any position. The governance of the monastery is in the hands of a committee called a 'small chapter' headed by the abbot, who is elected. The abbot in turn appoints three monks to the chapter and three others are elected from the members.

With its imposing physical structure St. Peter's Abbey rises above the prairie to provide an image of substance and achievement. It is a self-supporting community engaged in a variety of enterprises. The monk with his small room and the barest of personal possessions participates in a full ritual of prayer throughout the day. Because of the long-established practices of spiritual life, the tensions of group living are resolved through values and a terminology that is as old as occidental monasticism itself.

Monasticism in Western Canadian has survived because of its ties to the larger religious and ethnic community of which it is a part. The Trappist monastery in Manitoba was an outgrowth of the Francophone community of the province, and St. Peter's grew from the German Catholic settlement in that part of Saskatchewan. Because of its traditional emphasis on farming, monasticism fitted well with the agrarian settlement of the prairies and the pioneer rural communities that developed there.

Numerous other religious orders, especially those of nuns living in convents, provided the Catholic communities of Western Canada with an accepted and respected form of communalism. Through their operation of schools, hospitals, and other community facilities they gave communalism a presence it would otherwise never have had. Of course, that kind of communalism offered itself as a special kind of life. The community of goods was not suggested for believers as a whole, but only for the religious elite.

This was not the case with the Doukhobours, a sect that rose in Russia in the eighteenth century. They rejected the priesthood and the Orthodox Church structure and ritual. They too were part of the agrarian settlement of the West at the turn of the century. Their congregational approach to Christianity and their communal values demanded that they settle as groups. In 1899, 7,500 of the total Russian population of 30,000 made their way to Western Canada because of persecution in Russia over conscription and the requirement for an oath of allegiance to an earthly monarch.[40] They were assisted in their migration by the novelist Tolstoy and the English Quakers, who supported Doukhobour pacifism.

The Doukhobours took up land on the prairies under the "hamlet clause" of the Dominion Lands Act of 1872, which permitted the allocation of large blocs of land to groups wishing to settle as a community. One colony had 216 square miles; another had 540 square miles, and a third was made up of even-numbered mile square sections.[41] At the time, these colonies were the largest communal settlements in North America. Unfortunately, conflict arose between the Doukhobors and the government over the registration of land as freehold, which required an oath of allegiance. Within a few years of their arrival the Doukhobours were deprived of a substantial part of the land they had improved. Some agreed to live on single-family farms, while a majority, led by their charismatic leader, Peter Verigin, purchased land in the interior of southern British Columbia, where they lived communally. A small segment, known as the Sons of Freedom, became zealots who attacked other Doukhobours for what they considered apostasy. Their violent acts tended to discredit all Doubkhobours in the public eye.

The community in British Columbia that tried to live communally did succeed for some years with communal housing, farming, and industry, but the hostility of both provincial and federal governments over issues such as education, registration, and taxation eroded the economic base of their communalism. During the Depression they lost both industries and land, which they did not begin to recover until the 1950s. Today there are about 30,000 Doukhobours in Western Canada. Because of decades of running battles with the state, their communal life has been abandoned or eroded to such an extent that most Doukhobours see their faith as a private matter and communalism as impractical.

The history of Doukhobours in Western Canada shows how persecution can restrict and even destroy communal life. Because the Doukhobours were Slavs with a culture and language alien to Canada, their communal customs generated distrust and animosity. A major historical study of the sect in Canada concludes that "unrelenting hostility" from society and internal "disintegrative influences" were significant causes of their communal demise.[42] Doukhobours were fervent in their opposition to civil authority and they tended to use a confrontational style which aggravated delicate situations. This helped confirm the meaning of their name 'Spirit Wrestlers.' Their failure to maintain communalism is in sharp contrast to the success of the Hutterites, who have not given up communalism, not because they were more fervent but because they were more judicious in their dealings with the state and much less contentious among themselves.

The Hutterites came to Western Canada in 1918, at the end of the great agrarian settlement of the region. Like the Doukhobours and the monasteries, they were part of the rural civilization that characterized Western Canada from 1900 to the present period, and like the previous two communal groups, they were devout in their religious beliefs.

The Hutterites are an Anabaptist Christian sect who speak a Low-German dialect. The sect was organized in the 16th century in Moravia and named after its leader, Jacob Hutter. As a religious belief, their 450 year survival is not unusual, but the survival of their communalism for

93

such a long period most certainly is. Because of their nonconformist religious beliefs, their opposition to war and military service, and their communal lifestyle, the Hutterites have suffered from persecution throughout their history and have been driven to find refuge in one country after another. In the late eighteenth century they were accepted into Russia, where they began to rebuild, only to migrate to the United States in the 1870s when their military exemption was repealed. Forty-five years later they moved again—this time to Western Canada, because the Americans were persecuting them for their pacifist beliefs. Although they eventually re-established themselves in Montana and the Dakotas, most of them now reside in Western Canada.

The Hutterites began with an initial population of about 200 in 1528, which expanded rapidly during that century. Because of persecution their numbers diminished to less than 100 at the time of their last desperate migration to Russia. Approximately 1,000 immigrated to the United States and from that group there are now about 30,000 in North America, which makes them the continent's largest communal group.[43]

Not only are the Hutterites the largest communal group and the longest-surviving, they are also "the most successful in maintaining communal life."[44] They live in farm colonies, which they call 'bruderhofs.' Each bruderhof has a population of anywhere from 50 to 150 people, depending on the age of the colony. The youngest colonies tend to be the smallest. The basis of their community life and their community of goods is the Bible's description of the early Christian church, which was also important for the communalism of the monasteries and the Doukhobours. The Hutterites encourage segregation from the secular world. They maintain rural colonies, use their German dialect for internal communication, and wear an archaic dress that distinguishes them from everyone else. Similar features are found among other religious communalists such as Doukhobours and monks.

Each Hutterite is socialized to accept the collective will and to fit into the group. The result has been a minuscule rate of attrition—about two percent.[45] Because the Hutterites do not seek converts, their numbers increase through a high birth rate. This makes their way of life a total cradle to grave experience for their members. A lifetime of communalism means that each generation lives through the same patterns and with the same values. A high birth rate has ensured survival. If Hutterites had adopted the celibate practices of nineteenth century American religious communes, they most likely would have disappeared.

Life in the colony is strictly regimented. The Hutterites respect the family unit and provide separate accommodation for it, but the homes do not have kitchens because the colony eats communally in a single dining room. The day is divided into various parts, signalled by a bell that calls everyone to meals or to prayer. In the dining room, men, women, and children eat separately. Children are raised by their mothers until they go to kindergarten at about age three. At the age of six they go to 'English' school, which is situated in the colony and where they receive instruction in the approved government curriculum. Before and after school, children attend 'German' school, where they are instructed in the Hutterite language and religious beliefs. Hutterite children go to school only for the minimum time demanded by the state. Postsecondary education away from the colony is discouraged, if not forbidden. In this way the Hutterities fulfill their legal obligation and yet retain control over the education of their children.

Private property is insignificant in the colony. Each individual receives a small monthly allowance and children have a small box in which they lock up such personal possessions as a comb, a picture, etc. Everything else is for the use of members of the colony when it is needed. Men 'retire' at the age of fifty-five and the women at the age of forty-five. They remain active in the community but their tasks are lighter. The heavy farm work of the men and the major domestic cooking and laundry chores of the women fall on the shoulders of the younger generation, which is fully employed early on because of the limits on schooling.

Every fifteen years or so, a colony will subdivide to create a new colony, which often settles in an area some distance from the parent colony, depending on the availability of land. This subdividing keeps the colonies small enough to maintain a familial and familiar atmosphere. In those fifteen years, the parent colony must generate sufficient funds to purchase land and equipment to begin a new one. This is a major burden and requires a frugal lifestyle to ensure savings and efficient economic production to generate profit not only for the welfare of the parent colony but also for the welfare of future ones.

As an economic enterprise the Hutterite colony is basically a community of hard work. A colony may farm thousands of hectares, as well as operate chicken, cattle, and hog production. Unlike the kibbutz there is no industry in the colony and all capital has to be self-generated through the sale of either produce or land. Technologically the Hutterites try to be modern farmers. Because no one receives a salary, Hutterite colonies usually pay only corporate taxes. They are also reluctant to participate in various social security schemes.

Unlike Mondragon or the kibbutz federations, the Hutterites have no formal economic organization beyond the colony itself. There are no central co-operative services, no credit unions, no formalized system of inter-colony loans or centralized direction of Hutterite production.[46]

In spite of this, Hutterite colonies are considered excellent economic producers. One study has shown that the Hutterites of Manitoba, farming .83 percent of the province's farmland, generated 3.2 percent of provincial farm income.[47] A combination of frugality, hard work, and agricultural experience has ensured this high level of production. But it is the need for survival that is the ultimate motivator. "Ultimately the whole Hutterite way of life depends upon its economic structure," writes one authority, "for without this, they could not maintain their independent manner of living and Hutterite society would collapse."[48]

The colony focus of the Hutterites means that it is here that the main governing structure exists. The colony is ruled by an elected Board of Elders. The senior authorities in the colony are the minister or pastor, who leads the spiritual life, and the manager or colony boss, who is in charge of the economy. The colonies belong to one of three distinct groupings—the Schmiedeleut, the Dariusleut, and the Lehrerleut—each of which is headed by a council that meets annually. These three kinship groups are united in a church conference, which represents the Hutterites on legal and tax matters. Within this broad structure, property rights belong to each colony separately.

The main element in Hutterite survival is mobility. Because their prime allegiance is to God and their way of life, they are willing to move from country to country in search of peace. They have no nationalist interest whatsoever. This lack of attachment has allowed them to flee whenever a conflict between themselves and the wider society reaches a crisis point. In their sixty-five year history in Western Canada, the Hutterites have faced numerous attacks and restrictions which they have overcome through perseverance and adroit compromise. The province of Alberta has been particularly antagonistic in its legislation, restricting until recently sale of land to Hutterites. When this repressive legislation was enacted in the 1940s, the Hutterites simply established all their new colonies in neighbouring Saskatchewan.

This element of mobility also applies to their practice of branching off periodically to form new colonies. This method prevents a buildup of personality conflicts or antagonism and allows young or discontented members to found their own colony and go through the difficult pioneering experience.

The typical Anglo-American single-family farmer has felt threatened by Hutterites because he fears their competition for land and their growth. While the rural population of the West has declined dramatically, Hutterite population has increased and there remains a worry in some counties that they may become the majority. At present, Hutterite land ownership encompasses 1 percent of the total farm land in the prairie provinces and constitutes about 200 colonies. Although at present, governments are tolerant of Hutterites, there is no doubt that the underlying alienation between Hutterites and the larger society remains and can flare up at any time.[49]

Their historic willingness to branch off and move to more welcoming areas and the Hutterite propensity to avoid confrontation has served as a safety valve both for the general society and for the group itself. Their communal strength is bound up in their religious beliefs, their systematic socialization of the young, and their economy. But since the Hutterites are self-propagating and distrustful of converts, their communalism is not open to people in the wider society. They are a closed community. This is both a strength and a weakness. One the one hand it ensures control, while on the other hand it restricts general acceptance of their way of life. The contradiction of Hutterite communalism is that its very success is a threat.

The implications of this alienation are not serious when there is only a very small minority involved. But today, Hutterite numbers are greater than at any other time in their history and they are limited to a single region. At what point their growth will represent an issue for the wider society is unknown, but a reflection on their past history indicates a confrontation is likely, especially during wartime. What history shows is that the Hutterites will prevail by migrating to another place. By removing their colonies they preserve their communal way of life for themselves, but in the process they leave a communal void in the society they once inhabited.

In comparison with the region's religious communes, secular or political communalism in Western Canada has been at best a poor cousin and at worst, an abject failure. Both nineteenth and twentieth century examples illustrate this point.

In 1895 several Manitoba farmers, influenced by current English and American reform ideas, established the Harmony Industrial Association, which was to create a co-operative community at Hamona, Saskatchewan.[50] The group created an elaborate set of bylaws on the operation of their commune. Because of their efforts, the federal government amended the Dominion Lands Act in 1898 to allow group farming. The Doukhobors were the ones who first used the provision in a significant way. The Harmony community itself never exceeded 50 people and disbanded in 1900 with most of the members moving onto their own homesteads.

It was not till fifty years later that a new surge of co-op farming came about, again in Saskatchewan. The province had elected North America's first 'socialist' government in 1944. The Co-operative Commonwealth Federation (CCF) was a social democratic government which was susceptible to experimentation. The province already had a vital and successful Rochdale style co-op movement based on the wheat pool, the co-op stores, and credit unions. The economy of the province was solidly agricultural as was its social composition, so it was natural for its communalism to be agrarian. As well the radicalism of the Depression had not totally been erased by World War II.

In 1944 the new CCF government proposed that the Veteran's Land Act be amended to allow co-operative farming, which agricultural organizations in the province had favoured. In 1946, nineteen veterans, most of them single and young, launched a co-operative farm on 4,500 hectares of crown land near Matador. They were aided by some war assets, veteran's grants, and this major block of land courtesy of the CCF. The Matador community survives to this day. An examination of its forty year history provides insights into the development of secular communalism in Western Canada.

If one were to visit Matador today, one would find a small cluster of homes built in a semi-circle. Most of the homes are new and of some substance, with a few derelict buildings from the past such as the school house and the community hall. Eight families reside here and operate as the Matador Farm Pool.

Grey-haired and retired Lorne Dietrick, one of the founders, still lives at Matador and speaks fondly of its beginnings. "We were a poor man's co-op," he says. "We had only four homes for four married people and the rest of us lived in a dormitory with a paid housekeeper. This lasted until 1952."[51] Dietrick laments the loss of the early community spirit. The present generation has inherited a structure that the pioneers had to forge as best they could.

The Saskatchewan government was unable to convince the Federal Government to amend the Veterans' Land Act to allow group farming, so that land was eventually divided among the members and held as private property.[52] But the members continued to work the land co-operatively and to share profits. At one time the community had its own co-operative store and ran its own school. It built houses for the members, who were then responsible for the depreciation and insurance. Although there was no collective consumption, proximity to each other meant close community contact. The first crisis came in the mid-Fifties when the official ten year lease ran out and the farmers had to take the land as private owners. A number left the co-op. The second crisis came in the mid-Seventies when it was time to transfer the land to the next generation. Fortunately, there was an NDP government in power (successor to the CCF) and it had established a land bank scheme to aid young farmers. The members of Matador sold their land to the bank, which then leased it on good terms to their sons and so kept the co-op going.

Several other co-op farms were started but Matador has survived the longest. Victor Hay, who lived at Matador from 1959 to 1974, remembers the significant amount of free time each member had, the higher level of income generated by collective activity, and the superior amenities provided to members as compared to single-family farms in the neighbourhoood. He calls his years at Matador "a tremendous experience."[53]

However, the co-operative farm never developed into a realistic option for farmers in the province, and as an example of communalism it was very limited. In fact its closest parallel would be the Israeli moshav. There were simply too few co-op farms to reach a critical mass. The dominant co-operative ideology in the province was social democratic and even this moshav-style co-op farming was too socialist for most of the rural population. Co-op farms were never a major plank in CCF policy because of their lack of popularity and the limited amount of crown land that was available for homesteading. A major movement would have required large-scale funding to convert private land to social property. Community distrust, resistance by the state to collective land tenure, and the isolation of farm co-ops in a sea of private farms undermined their development.

In a social environment historically committed to the single family farm and private property, the concept of group farming was too alien for most to contemplate. There was no overriding force that pushed for it. Western Canadians never put into power a political movement that made co-operative farms a basic feature of social life. And considering the role of religious authority in maintaining religious communes, it would be fair to conclude that only if there had been an overriding political authority supporting it, would secular communalism have been able to sustain itself and expand.

THE IDEOLOGY OF COMMUNALISM

If one were to use the criterion of longevity as a mark of successful communalism, religious communes rank high and secular communes rank low. The main reason for this is that communalism is more easily maintained in religious communes. For example, religious communes emphasize otherworldliness and the importance of the spiritual over the material, which encourages the isolation needed by communes. Secular communes, meanwhile, practise separation yet preach social change. The religious communes tend to see society as unredeemable, while secular communes see it as worthy of change. In the matter of the community of goods, religious communes see this as a vehicle to achieve higher values, but secular communes see it as the highest good. The result is that religious communes subordinate communal life to their religious quest and so do not burden it with ultimate value as do secular communes.

On the issue of charismatic leadership, religious communes are much more comfortable with an authoritarian structure than are the secular. Secular communes usually profess some sort of democratic and socialist ideology which is opposed to the hierarchical system in which religious communes operate. Yet authoritarianism seems vital to long-term communal survival. Of course, religious communes have some system of voting and are strong on egalitarian production and consumption but their disciplined hierarchical command structure is more stable than that of secular communes.

Another advantage religious communes have over secular ones is that religious dissent is more acceptable in capitalist societies than political dissent. Since the goal of religious communes is not the transformation of society, the powers that be and the general population feel less threatened. Only when communalism is an economic threat or involves a rejection of social obligations such as military service does confrontation develop. Kenneth Rexroth pointed to the grave problem of confrontation when he wrote of the Hutterites:

> Had they been combative and indulged in massive confrontation as a tiny minority in the midst of a world which was often bitterly antagonistic, and at best, indifferent, they would have long since been destroyed.[54]

It is clear that communalism survives only when it is tolerated by the state or has sufficient backing in the wider society. Monasticism is part of the larger Catholic community and is protected by that community. In contrast, the Doukhobours had no such community support and their communalism was destroyed.

Communalism requires a powerful ideology such as religion to ensure commitment and cohesion; it needs a carefully screened membership; and its leadership must be able to create a successful economy.[55] Religious communes achieve these goals more easily. The secular communes of the nineteenth and twentieth centuries were poor at selecting members and deficient ideologically. But it is not just firmness and clarity of one's beliefs that make the difference. It is the belief itself.

Communalism needs an inward-oriented and self-contained reality to maintain its practice, but secular socialist ideology is outward-oriented and interactive with history and social process. Secular communes have yet to overcome this problem.

But it is unfair to describe communalism as 'utopian' because so many communes were shortlived. A number of years ago, the sociologist Henrik Infield wrote:

> The term 'utopianism' has been abused to a point where the value of its further use has become debatable. Its continued application to experimental communities is merely confusing. Why classify as 'utopian' a community life like the Hutterites which has existed now for more than four hundred years and is still growing?[56]

Communalism cannot be written off as utopian and therefore impractical because it has been successful. Interestingly, the most successful communes are those that rejected the concept of their commune as a heaven on earth, and insisted it was only a waystation to something higher.

Comparing communalism to other co-operative traditions allows one to assess its contribution to co-operative development. Communalism, while being the furthest from the liberal democratic co-op on private property and on the number of people involved, is nearest to it in terms of voluntary membership. That the two polarities of co-operation should share this feature is indicative of the flexibility of co-operative principles and the importance of free association within capitalist societies, where communes and liberal democratic co-ops exist.

What communalism shares with Marxist collectives is an emphasis on communal production, but Marxist collectives generally do not encourage communal consumption, which is somehow viewed as anti-socialist. Likewise communalism is not class oriented and views its impact on history as one of example rather than the manipulation of political power. The small and discrete nature of communes is not of interest to Marxism, which is attuned to the development of a mass society and appropriate institutions for everyone.

The greatest similarity lies with the socialist communities. Here, values overlap between the two traditions, but the socialist communities reject the marginality and tendency to withdraw which marks communes. Their nationalism integrates them with the society in which they live and whose development they share fully. Socialist co-operative communities have succeeded as a social vanguard primarily because they have overcome the isolation of secular communes.

101

The challenge for communalism is to make itself work for both religious and secular manifestations. To date secular communes have not been able to overcome their basic contradiction of withdrawal from society and the need to change it. It would seem that political communalism is destined to remain a shortlived, experimental mode of life that releases its members into more widely accepted forms of organization as the communes of the Sixties did, or else becomes a socialist co-operative community like the kibbutz. Only religious communes have been able to maintain lasting communities in their own right.

A SUMMARY OF THE HISTORICAL TRADITION

Our survey of co-operation indicates that co-operative institutions are found in every part of the world and that they range from low-involvement liberal democratic co-ops to high-intensity communes. In some places they receive no more than benign neglect from society, while in other countries they are at the forefront of state policy and serve as a cornerstone of social and economic organization. Co-operation is not only a broad phenomenon but an expanding one. It is constantly generating new forms to deal with evolving conditions.

When faced with such an array of organizational forms, one may feel overwhelmned and so be tempted to focus on differences in order to make sense of it all rather than seek a common identity. Yet commonality is where the essence of co-operation resides. It is in the shared features that we find co-operation's essential nature and the source of all new co-operative forms.

All co-operatives share two basic features that ensure their membership in a single family. First is their idealistic goal of ending exploitative relations through self-help group action. Second is their pragmatic goal of successful economic activity. The interplay of idealism and pragmatism is the basic dialect that propels co-operatives to new levels and creates the pattern that evolves from utopian phase through movement phase to systems phase.

From our study of various kinds of mutual aid we can conclude that the original ideal of a co-operative commonwealth or a society operating on co-operative principles has not been achieved. This has meant that co-operatives have been subordinate to either a broader political ideology as has happened in communust countries or to a nonco-operative economic system such as capitalism. This minority position has forced adaptability and flexibility onto co-ops and made them open to change.

What is clear from our review of the four historical traditions is that the only successful co-operative forms are those that end up as co-operative systems. The isolated single phenomenon is headed for death. Only when co-ops replicate themselves and interact with each other do they develop and grow. This is true of liberal democratic co-ops that generate second and third tier structures with only institutional membership; it is also true of factories jointly established by kibbutzim; and it is true of Hutterite colonies which use each other for marriage and economic assistance. It is only when a co-op becomes part of a larger co-operative system that it can even entertain the possibility of long-term survival.

Differences between types of co-ops result from their subordination to the political and economic cultures in which they exist and from which they take some of their characteristics. When these political economies are in conflict, as are the communist and capitalist ones, the co-ops in these systems adopt the conflict as their own. For example, a member of a Chinese commune would be taught that a liberal democratic co-op was an inferior form of co-operation because of its respect for private property, while a member of a wheat pool in North America would probably view communal life as an affront to his individual entrepreneurship and the sanctity of the family unit. This battle is more a product of the ideologies in which these co-ops live than co-op principles themselves. It is the capitalist influence in liberal democratic co-ops that produces opposition to communist collectives, while it is the Marxist influence that produces a condemnation of liberal democratic co-ops. The following statement by the Hutterite leader Michael Entz indicates how sensitive is the issue of similarity between one tradition and the other and how much easier it is to emphasize differences.

> There's two kinds of communism in the world. There's a Christian communism and there's a secular communism, like...in Russia. Their communism preaches that what's thine is mine...where we believe that what is mine is thine.[57]

Once we have separated the co-operative ideology or values from the political ideologies with which they co-exist and which dominate them, we can then seek out the common ground that underlies the whole historical tradition. There are five such principles that are shared by the four traditions: non-exploitation, democracy, utilitarianism, co-operation over competition, and group self-determination. A sampling from each tradition will indicate how these principles are practised in each.

A credit union is a good example of a liberal democratic co-op in the

Rochdale tradition. Credit unions are created to provide an alternative to capitalist banks, whose goal is profit at the expense of its customers. The credit union operates on a democratic one person/one vote principle. It is created to provide financial assistance and services that may not be available or are too costly. It also allows the members of a credit union to determine the direction of their institution and how it will serve them.

A Chinese commune is meant to end exploitative relations found in capitalist societies by developing equality among members through the sharing of economic returns. The commune operates through consciousness-raising discussion and democratic voting. The utilitarian purpose of the commune is an increase in production and living standards. Although state production norms are established and party policy generated at the top, control of the commune's surplus and its division among members is still determined by the group.

In a kibbutz egalitarianism in production and consumption ensures non-exploitation of members. Policy is set by the members by voting and by consensus. The purpose of the kibbutz is to use its collective structure to build Israel and to further socialism. The individual gains when the group prospers just as he does in the credit union and the Chinese commune. Co-operation among members is the norm. And of course the kibbutz is self-determining on many issues of daily life.

A Hutterite colony has no owner-worker exploitative structure. People work for the benefit of everyone and share equally in the results. The community of goods ensures equality and the democratic process is respected in electing the leadership. Co-operation among members is the norm and competition is dealth with severely. Although colonies share a common religious faith and tradition, they view themselves as self-determining not only in economic matters but also in terms of religious self-government. It is part of their Anabaptist tradition.

Of course the five principles are not observed perfectly. There are problems in each tradition. In the kibbutz it is hired labour; in the Hutterite colony it is the subordinate role of women; in the Chinese commune it is the overwhelming power of state policy; and in the credit union it is individualism and private property. But in spite of these failures, the basic thrust of co-operation is maintained and respected in theory if not always in practice.

These principles are the mutual bond that links traditions into a single yet scattered and often feuding family of institutions. That tradition also provides an insight into the basic factors needed to ensure institutional viability. First, co-operatives must be answers to specific and often intense social and economic needs. Without this driving force, co-operative organizations simply do not come about. The Rochdale model itself was a response to the need for less costly and purer food for workers. The Chinese Indusco co-ops were a response to the Japanese invasion. Since these socio-economic needs appear at different times and places, the forms that co-operation adopts is as varied as the milieus in which they arise.

Second, co-operative formation is dependent on idealism. The Rochdale pioneers were out to create a utopian co-operative community when they established their store. And the kibbutzim were offered as a new way of life without exploitation of their fellow man. In a real sense, every co-operative tradition is an exercise in hope and the vision of a higher level of life is fundamental to this.

Third, every co-operative form must be adaptable to the dominant system in which it resides. If a kolkhoz were not integrated ideologically into the Soviet system and the mechanisms of a command economy it would fail. If the Hutterite commune did not participate in the marketplace economy of Western Canada it would cease to exist. Adaptability means initially that a co-op cannot have a form that is considered threatening to the dominant system in any fundamental way.

The historical tradition teaches us that co-operation occurs when there are real needs that can be met; when the co-operative project is motivated by high ideals; and when its organizational form is adaptable to a specific situation. These three conditions of viability can be rolled into one statement: co-ops have to be historically relevant to survive. And that relevance is a result of their being part of larger forces at work in their society and whose product they are.

In Part Two of this book we will explore what historical forces exist in Canada that favour a new kind of co-operative and how the three basic conditions of co-operative success can be met.

THE SEARCH FOR COMMUNITY

Part Two:
SOCIAL
COOPERATIVES

Chapter Six:
THE GENERAL THEORY

ISSUES IN THE GENERAL THEORY OF CO-OPERATION

Because there are four distinct traditions in co-operation, discussion has arisen among them concerning the nature of co-operation and the principles on which its various organizational forms ought to rest. These issues have been debated for some time and the position various traditions have taken on these issues has come to define their co-operative ideology.

There are about a dozen issues that divide the traditions. First there is the question of what constitutes a co-operative and what kind of organization has the right to call itself a co-op. Second, there is a debate between those who prefer unifunctional co-operatives and those who favour co-operative communities. Third, there is the issue of whether a co-op ought to be an internationally applicable model or a purely national one. Fourth, there is a discussion on whether egalitarianism or simple democratic voting is necessary for equality. Fifth, there are partisans of voluntary organizations and those who believe state direction is crucial. Sixth, there are exponents of co-operation as an all-class phenomenon and those who see it as an integral part of the class struggle. Seventh, there are supporters of centralized authority and those who see decentralization as essential for co-operative development. Eighth there is an argument between proponents of co-operatives as evolutionary and those who see them as having a revolutionary role. This argument is usually part and parcel of the debate on whether co-ops ought to be associated with socialism. Ninth, there is the debate about the preference of rural or urban environments for co-ops. And finally, there is the discussion over whether the best way of developing co-operation is through expanding established forms or by initiating new ones.

The first issue—what is a co-op?—results from the variety of organizational types which people have created to help each other by pooling resources. Jenny Thornley, in a book on worker co-ops, describes a co-op as "a particular kind of firm which has grown up around a set of ideological beliefs in response to external economic and social circumstances."[1] That is a wide open definition which allows some writers to call the kibbutz "in many ways the most remarkable co-operative in the world."[2] It also allows others to describe the kolkhoz as "co-operative farming of the Soviet type" and "a semi-independent co-operative organization."[3] This broad approach has been the basis of this book but it certainly is not a universally accepted one.

Lazlo Valko, a partisan of liberal democratic co-ops, stands firm on Rochdale rules and denounces the communist collectives as "forced collectives" which cannot be honored with the name co-op. But even he is willing to admit that "there is no general theory which can be pronounced as an exclusive and consistent philosophy of co-operation."[4] Historically, the liberal democratic tradition has tried to use the Rochdale rules—one member/one vote; limited return on capital; equitable distribution of surplus; voluntary, open membership; co-operative education; and co-operation among co-operatives—as a definition of what constitutes a co-op. In its 1967 report on co-operative principles, the International Co-operative Alliance stated that it was its responsibility to consider the essential characteristics of co-operatives, that these characteristics were six of the Rochdale rules, and that there was such a thing as a 'cooperative sector' as opposed to private enterprise and a state sector.[5]

By adopting the ICA approach , the four traditions have a reasonable claim to belong to a co-operative sector of an economy, that is, one that is neither owned by the state nor by a capitalist enterprise. They can also claim that they follow most or all of the Rochdale rules and that in many cases they go well beyond what is required by these rules. Alex Laidlaw wrote in 1980 that "the architecture of co-operation is far from perfect" and in his report to the ICA he called for a clarification of co-operation in terms of fundamental precepts rather than just operating rules.[6] He felt that this would allow room for a wide range of ideologies to exist under the co-op umbrella. Another Canadian expert, Jack Craig, talked about the variety of ideologies and organizational forms that can be found among co-ops.[7] The French scholar Henri Desroches has even gone so far as to raise doubts about whether we can even speak of a "traditional co-operative model."[8] While Rochdale is considered the "first modern co-operative," Louis Smith points out that it came from the desire to create a utopian community.[9] To reduce co-operation to the workings of a retail store would be an impoverishment of the concept.

One way in which the liberal democratic tradition could continue to hold fast to its definition of what is a co-op and yet allow the existence of a wider, more diverse co-operative tradition would be to use the indigenous terminology for the non-liberal democratic forms rather than the word ''co-op.'' A credit union is a co-operative, while a kibbutz is not a co-operative but a co-op community. The distinction between a co-operative and a co-operative community seems minor but it does allow us to let the liberal democratic tradition have exclusive use of 'co-operative' as an institutional-legal term, and yet allows the use of co-operative as an adjective or modifier. Where it is used as an adjective it indicates that the core is 'community,' while in the term 'worker co-op' it is a liberal democratic co-op that is the core.

The second issue concerns the unifunctional versus multifunctional co-ops. The single function co-operative is typical of the liberal democratic tradition, but the other three traditions—Marxist, socialist, communalist—emphasize an all-inclusive kind of co-operation. In these traditions community control is more important than private property. The organizational form that is created deals with various problems and issues under the umbrella of a single community structure. But the liberal democratic tradition likes to divide co-operatives by function and argues that this approach has allowed co-ops to proliferate in capitalist economies. However, the supporters of the community approach respond that co-operative communities can also maintain themselves within capitalism and that community offers a way of life rather than a way of doing busines.

It is clear that co-operative community does offer its members a fuller and deeper co-operative experience because it operates on many levels, but it is equally clear that in capitalist economies co-operative community is definitely a very minor phenomenon compared to liberal democratic co-ops, which are everywhere. In a sense what we have in the unifunctional/multifunctional debate is a trade-off. Co-operative community does offer depth of experience, but only for a limited number of people. Rochdale co-ops offer a shallow experience, yet touch millions of people. Only in the command economies of Marxist states does the multifunctional co-op touch the lives of millions.

The third issue is that of international versus national models of co-operation. Again the liberal democratic tradition has created a model that is applicable to any market economy. So these co-ops, involving hundreds of millions of people, can be found in every continent in the world, while co-operative communities tend to be restricted to national models. The only exception to this is the communal tradition, which exists outside single national boundaries. Since both models touch the lives of hundreds of millions, size is not an issue in favouring one over the other. The strength of national models comes from their reflection of local conditions and a local community. The strength of liberal democratic co-ops lies in their universal applicability.

The issue of egalitarian versus democratic objectives for cooperation is important because it separates the liberal democratic tradition from the other three. All the traditions operate democratically on a one person/one vote basis but the liberal democratic orientation is not a move toward egalitarianism because of its promotion of private holdings. In the other traditions it is the emphasis on community and on social property that encourages equality. Of course, there is substantial variation from one tradition to another, but Marxists, socialists, and communalists pay theoretical allegiance to creating equality in consumption and production, which liberal democrats do not.

It is the sense of fraternity, of the need for co-operative relationships at all levels that infuses the co-operative project in these traditions with egalitarian values. It is a more radical sense of equity and justice than is found in the liberal democratic tradition. The egalitarian approach to co-operation is one that challenges the private property and marketplace orientation of the liberal democratic tradition and cannot be disassociated from those social theories which aim to reduce or eliminate class differences based on individual wealth.

The argument over the voluntary versus nonvoluntary nature of co-operation is an argument between those who oppose state intervention and those who favour it. The voluntarists claim that only freely entered relationships are genuine, meaningful, and effective. An organization cannot be democratic until it is voluntary. The proponents of state intervention point out that the government must express the interests of the dispossessed economically and socially and that a popular government, especially after a revolution, must guide social development in such a manner that the defeated classes will not regain control.

Voluntarism is basic to the liberal democratic, socialist, and communalist traditions but is weak in the Marxist sphere. The record shows that the voluntary principle is the dominant one and that even the marxist tradition has had to pay lip service to it when describing forced collectivization.

In the liberal democratic and communalist traditions class consciousness and class struggle are not part of co-operation, at least officially. ''The co-operative movement is not at all a class movement,'' writes Lazlo Valko.[10] Yet the Marxist and socialist traditions consider co-operation as an economic tool of the peasants and workers. Co-operatives are not of much use to capitalists or the bourgeoisie. Bill Brugger in his study of postrevolutionary China showed how co-operatives were instituted by the Communist Party to destroy the old rural class structure by putting the majority of peasants in power over the few wealthier ones.[11] This was certainly true of collectivization under Stalin, who claimed the kolkhoz was created to destroy the power of the wealthier peasants.

Although liberal democratic co-ops and communes in capitalist countries are open to all classes and do not engage in class struggle, the services they provide are of interest to those, like farmers and workers, who have little economic control. For unionists forming credit unions and farmers building producer co-ops, co-operation is a method of increasing their power. In this sense co-operation is class-based. Whether it was the Desjardins movement in Quebec, or the Antigonish movement in Nova Scotia, or the wheat pools of the West, liberal democratic co-ops appealed to those classes which felt exploited by the system. One writer has described how even the conservative liberal democratic tradition in Britain arose ''out of conditions of hardship or disillusion caused by capitalist development.[12]

The debate over centralization versus decentralization exists in each tradition. The present systems phase of liberal democratic co-ops points to a highly centralized mechanism in which ever larger units are developed. The tendency to centralize decision-making is also strong in the economies of China and Russia, but this is balanced in the marxist tradition by Yugoslav self-management. The socialist tradition remains on the decentralized side of the scale but that is becoming increasingly difficult to maintain as the evolution of Mondragon and the kibbutzim has shown. So it remains for the communalist tradition to emphasize decentralization. It is here that independent decision-making is strongest and where economic life is locally controlled.

In the decentralized model direct democracy is possible while large-scale sophisticated economic organization is not. The centralized model allows economy of scale but only limited imput from the grassroots. Whenever centralization occurs there is a reaction which calls for smaller, more manageable and more personal forms of co-operation.

The division between the evolutionists and the revolutionists separates the Marxists from the liberal democrats and the communalists and leaves the socialists sitting on the fence. The Marxist tradition makes co-operation a result of a revolutionary process, while the liberal democrats and the communalists, especially the religious ones, view their movements as peaceful and evolutionary. What gives the socialist tradition a foot in both camps is its nationalist side. The kibbutz was an integral part of the Zionist program to create a state of Israel, and Mondragon is an integral part of Basque nationalism, while the ujamaa village was conceived as an expression of African nationalism.

What divides the two sides is the political component. In the liberal democratic and communalist traditions politics takes a back seat, but in the Marxist and socialist ones it is either an equal partner or in the forefront.

The discussion over whether co-operatives are socialist depends on what one means by socialism and that is certainly an ongoing controversy. If one says that socialism is state ownership, then co-ops are not socialist. But if one defines socialism as a noncapitalist system of democratic and equitable self-management and ownership then co-operatives are socialist. The word "socialist" and the word "co-operative" have co-existed, but it has been an uneasy alliance. As Robert Oakeshott, a supporter of worker co-ops in Britain, has pointed out, socialists have emphasized public ownership and trade union power rather than co-operation.[13] And in communist countries co-operatives are held to be a lower form of equitable relations than that created by state ownership.

If we consider co-operation and socialism as simply anticapitalist ideologies, then they share a common understanding, but if we digress into all the schools of socialism and all the strategies of achieving socialism we get bogged down in a morass of conflicting viewpoints. So on this question, it is best to be aware of the historical connection between co-operation and socialism in the various traditions, but not portray that association as always mutually supportive.

The final debate among the traditions concerns those who favour the exponential development of what already exists and those who favour striking out in new directions. When the Canadian co-operator Alex Laidlaw wrote in 1981 that "there will be many new forms and kinds of co-operatives which are not generally known today" he was speaking primarily of the Rochdale model, but being a person of global interests he could see how different political economies had created their own co-operative forms.[14] In each tradition there are those whose main goal is the stable development of that tradition and its reproduction in as many areas as possible. In a very real sense the traditions cannot go beyond themselves. For example, liberal democratic co-ops cannot form co-operative communities of the socialist kind but they can apply Rochdale rules in new areas such as housing and employment.

The impetus for new co-operative forms in each tradition comes from outside the power structure. It is on the periphery that new ideas and feelings of dissatisfaction begin to take form and it is at this outside circle that new developments are debated and pushed toward realization. John Jordan has pointed out how those "less encumbered by commitments to the present state of affairs" can launch new beginings.[15] Although there are opportunities for evolution within each tradition, a totally new tradition can come about only with a new political economy.

ISSUES IN THE CANADIAN CO-OPERATIVE MOVEMENT

Since the Canadian co-operative sector is part of the liberal democratic tradition, it shares in the general problems encountered by this tradition in its systems phase. These problems are: decreasing member involvement, increasing bureaucratic control and the growth of a managerial class, consolidation of co-ops into ever larger units and their centralization, and a lowering of ideological commitment to co-operation among members.

Some of these issues have been raised in recent years by the Canadian co-operative system itself, which has been engaged in a wide-ranging evaluation of where it is going and the difficulties it faces. In the early Eighties the Co-operative Future Directions Project at York University in Toronto was funded by the established co-op system to do an analysis of its present and future state. The project produced an extensive series of monographs by Canadian academics and concluded with a major summary published in 1982 under the title *Patterns and Trends of Canadian Co-operative Development*. The study confirmed that Canadian co-ops are well into the systems phase and it pointed out that Canadian co-operatives now have "an operating style in which membership does not fundamentally matter."[16] It also criticized the co-op sector for being rigid and moribund in terms of developing new areas of co-operative endeavour.

This critique was discussed within the system and its impact is evident in the 1984 Report of the National Task Force on Co-operative Development, which was prepared by leading personalities in the system. The purpose of the report was to lobby the federal and provincial governments for increased aid to the co-op sector and for legislative changes that would make the sector more competitive in the marketplace. The report called for initiatives in developing new worker, health, and fisheries co-ops, which indicates that the system was trying to respond to earlier criticism.

The main thrust of the report was the portrayal of the co-op system in a positive way to outsiders so that the system's suggestions "to strengthen and extend the co-operative system" would be accepted by the government.[17] To this end it concluded that membership is rising, that democratic control was alive and well, that the co-op sector is a potent economic force nationally, and that the sector is growing. It is certainly interesting to compare this portrait with the one painted earlier by the academics.

The difference between the two is understandable because the goal of the academics was to analyze and raise questions, while the goal of the co-op leadership was to interpret the status quo in a positive light. It is not the differences in what each report calls problems that is the real issue. The real issue is the system's need to turn outward to government for expansion and renewal rather than turn inward to the membership. A small but significant example of this trend is the situation faced by the Alberta credit union system in 1984. Because of real estate losses due to the collapse of the Alberta economy, the credit union system was under intense pressure. Withdrawals increased dramatically as members rushed to save their funds. Finally the provincial government had to step in to guarantee the system and in turn placed its own people in control.

The lack of member loyalty is a symptom of the alienation in liberal democratic co-ops. O. A. Turnbull, former head of the Co-op College of Canada and former Minister of Co-operatives in Saskatchewan put it bluntly when he commented "The whole concept of membership is being eroded."[18]

The causes of this erosion are severalfold. First, there is the increasing importance and dominance of second and third tier co-op institutions, which have no human members. Alex Laidlaw commented on this in the mid-Seventies when he pointed out that "tens of thousands of co-operative members in Canada are served directly by a third-level organization for which they are twice removed in respect of control."[19] Second, there is the ever-increasing size of Canadian co-ops themselves. Continued consolidation and centralization has meant bigger and bigger institutions with the alienation which size creates. In 1982 *Patterns and Trends* made the observation that the average credit union membership stood at 2,000 with only 10 roles for active members or a ratio of 1 to 200.[20] Only in the newly established housing co-op sector is direct democracy wide-spread.

When participation is limited, the nature of co-operative democracy changes. Since the main concern of large commercial co-operative organizations is their interaction and relationship with the total economic environment, that is, market share, their interest in the democratic process is limited.[21] Formal lip service is paid to democracy but the structure of the system encourages nondemocratic operation.

Related to the deterioration of member participation and control is the issue of decreasing ideological commitment to co-operative philosophy. Since the liberal democratic tradition requires the least amount of commitment of the four traditions, it is not surprising to find ideology at a low level. Continued decline poses a threat to the very identity of co-ops themselves. *Patterns and Trends* noted that utilitarian goals had become paramount in Canadian co-ops and it warned that a lack of perceived difference between co-operatives and capitalist institutions is a danger to genuine co-operative development.[22]

The anti-ideological nature of the systems phase means that the kind of energy and ideals expressed in the utopian and movement phases has been put aside and replaced with a self-centred pragmatism. Member loyalty is not based on ideological commitment but upon personal benefit. As soon as a capitalist enterprise offers a better deal, the member is willing to switch. Ideological commitment creates a bond of association that goes beyond self-benefit and involves selfsacrifice. When co-operation is reduced to personal fiscal benefits and nothing more, then it is doomed to imitating capitalist practice.

Of course, the system regrets the lack of commitment and continues to agonize over the problem, but it is unable to move out of the systems phase. The lack of ideological commitment among members is part and parcel of the systems phase. It cannot be wished away. Only with a resurgence of utopian ideals and the founding of wholly new co-ops can the spirit come to life. Skip Kutz of the Co-op College is right when he says that "there is no missionary zeal in today's co-op movement," but it would be fair to add that the system's goal of self-maintenance and management precludes such a possibility.[23]

This does not mean that there are not repeated calls for renewal from within the system. For example, Marcel Laflamme, writing about Quebec's four million members, decries the lack of co-operative education and makes suggestions on how the system might become a social movement once again.[24] But history shows that the cycle of utopian-movement-systems phases is the route of fundamental change. In every case it is grassroots enthusiasm and idealistic leadership striking off in new directions which gives birth to new institutions. It is not the system that does this. Dr. Darin-Drabkin's description of the origins of the kibbutz are a reminder of that reality:

> Out of a mere handful, a group of a few individuals grew a vast project embracing more than 200 settlements...dedicated to realizing some of the highest aspirations and ideals of mankind.[25]

The idealistic impulse that launches a utopian phase involves a return to first principles. When leaders of a system attempt to do this they get away from their prime role of managing immediate interests. On the periphery these obligations do no exist. Here the problems facing co-ops and problems facing society in general interact and produce change.

In the conclusion to Part One I wrote that "co-operation occurs when there are real needs that can be met; when the co-operative project is motivated by high ideals; and when its organizational form is suited to a specific situation." This chapter discusses contemporary needs; the next chapter discusses basic ideals; and the final chapter outlines the organizational form that this new co-op could take.

RATIONALE FOR A NEW CO-OPERATIVE

The major socio-economic issue of the 1980s in Western Canada is unemployment. It shares this problem with the rest of Canada but considering the boom that the region experienced in the 1970s, unemployment at double and even triple the earlier rate is a social trauma. In the period after 1981 Canada underwent a recession from which it had not yet recovered in 1985. Although central Canada had a minor recovery in 1983-84, Western Canada did not experience any such recovery till 1985. Its resource extraction economy continued to suffer from low commodity prices. The region went from a period of high inflation to one of deflation. In the 1982-85 period, Alberta, the flagship province of the region, was beset by thousands of home foreclosures, business bankruptcies, and farm discontent. The province had an unemployment rate of 12 percent going into 1985 and predicitons of double-digit unemployment until the early 1990s.[26]

The Economic Council of Canada stated in 1983 that "unemployment has been stretched to the bounds of social endurance."[27] And in a statement on contemporary Canadian issues, the Catholic Bishops of Canada stated in 1983 that unemployment was "the number one problem."[28] A clergyman who works with the destitute in Edmonton said that he was seeing "the image of the Depression" in the faces of the men with whom he was dealing.[29] Canadian unemployment had risen from 7 percent in 1975 to 12 percent in 1985. This trend indicated that unemployment was a longterm phenomenon.

The economy was forcing people onto the unemployment rolls and lowering the incomes of those working. Women suffered from lowpaying jobs. The service sector with its predominance of minimum-wage occupations and low-skill occupations was growing as was part-time employment. Government make-work projects only added to the new poverty that the economy was forcing on people.

In the United States, which has experienced rapid technological change, 2.7 million goods-producing jobs were lost in the 1982 recession but only half of those jobs were recovered when things improved.[30] The whole manufacturing and secondary industry sector is being revolutionized away from human employment toward robots and computers, a trend that began in the Seventies but accelerated dramatically in the 1980s.[31]

In Western Canada unemployment and underemployment have

118

become a fact of life. Except for social democratic Manitoba, the West has witnessed a deep erosion of union power, working class income, and the creation of an economic reality in which only the two wage earner family is able to produce the income necessary to maintain a household.[32]

Alex Laidlaw made the observation in 1980 that "co-operatives generally are unable to act as strong agents of political change. Their main role is in the field of economies rather than political change."[33] He was right. Economic change is the mandate of co-ops and in Western Canada the mandate must focus on unemployment as once it focused on farmers. A co-operative that deals with this social issue is relevant and necessary.

The second major problem of the 80s is the reduction in the standard of living of the majority of people due to cutbacks in public and social services because of government restraint programs and privatization. Canada now has a predominance of conservative governments whose goal is the reduction of benefits to citizens. In British Columbia it is education that is being savaged; in Alberta it is health care; and in Saskatchewan it is social assistance that is being cut. In the final years of the federal Liberals social spending did not grow as fast as the expansion of the economy.[34]

Anyone who has lived in Canada during the five years from 1980 to 1985 needs no reminder of the fundamental attack on the welfare state, which has added to the burden placed on workers. Only a co-op that deals with this erosion in social services can expect to answer contemporary needs.

Besides unemployment and social service cutbacks, there are several other issues that a new co-operative would have to face. First, there is the changed nature of Western Canada's economy in the Sevenites. In that decade the engines of economic growth were resource extraction industries that shipped oil, natural gas, uranium, potash, timber, and coal. In an inflationary period the value of these commodities was high and increasing. In today's market, their value has gone down. Agriculture which had once been the prime mover of the region's economy was no longer the leading edge. In fact agricultural commodity prices remained depressed into the 80s and farmers were able to borrow only against inflated land values. These values have since tumbled.

Even though agriculture was no longer the main vehicle of economic growth in the region, the new resource extraction industries have turned out to be no different in their impact. They are all primary sector industries based on export and world commodity prices.[35] The region began as a primary producer during the fur trade period, remained so during the agrarian period, and continues so today. There has been no change in the region's relationship to either central Canada or the U.S. As Pro-

119

fessor John Conway of the University of Regina has written: "The West's economic place in Confederation, in all essential aspects, remains unchanged...The West was still a hewer of wood and a drawer of water."[36]

Historically, the region has resented this role of primary producer and the boom and bust cycle that it entails, but it has been unable to develop the secondary industry and economic diversification that would help it out of its structural problems. In the period of the fur trade it was London and Montreal that were dominant. In the agrarian period it was central Canada's National Policy that was denounced as unfair and during the 1970s Western separatism arose on the energy question.[37] However, none of the provincial governments was able to alter the system and its dependent relationship on American markets and central Canadian political dominance.

A new co-operative for the region would have to address this issue, examine the causes of the problem, and work for the industrialization of the region. Only in this way would it be responding to the underlying problems that have kept the region's economy subservient and dependent.[38]

The boom of the 1970s created a new social reality in the West, which made the region primarily urban and working class. The rural population and the farm economy has lost its clout.[39] In Canada only 5 percent of the population is employed in agriculture.[40] In the United States, which is the trend-setter in North American farming, only 3.3 percent of the population lives on farms.[41] Since Western Canada is a sparsely populated area, with most of its population living in the southern half of the prairie provinces, rural depopulation is a trend that has made the West's urban centres preeminent. Any new co-op would have to orient itself to this urban, working-class reality.

The focus on urban life would mean that the new co-op would have to deal with the changing nature of social relations. The ever increasing numbers of divorced couples, single-parent families, and children outside the traditional family structure, and demands for women's equality at home and in the workplace are all part of the new social reality of life in the region and a new co-op would have to see itself as an response to this situation.

To summarize: a new co-operative for the region would be one that aims to create employment in response to unemployment; that promotes social control over the means of production in answer to privatization of the public sector; that contributes to the industrialization and economic diversification of the region; that takes up the challenge of providing social security and lost public sector services to people; that encourages economic and social equality for both sexes and lessens the growing gap between income levels and services available to different classes.

There are no co-operatives in Western Canada at present that deal fundamentally with these social needs. Nor are there any co-ops that tackle the problems facing liberal democratic co-ops in their systems phase. Only a new co-operative would be able to focus on both the external problems in society and the internal problems of co-ops. This new co-op would have to provide answers to both constituencies. And it could do so by returning to first principles and taking a stand on the issues that have divided co-operation during this century. When this new co-op has articulated its values and has shown how these values meet the needs of society in general and co-ops in particular, it can then propose an organizational form that responds to the contemporary historical situation.

THE SEARCH FOR COMMUNITY

Chapter Seven:
THE IDEOLOGY

FUNDAMENTAL PRINCIPLES

"Every organization or institution is built, first of all, on ideas and concepts of what people believe and are willing to stand for...it is from these ideas they take their direction."[1] This statement by one of Canada's most outstanding co-operative leaders indicates the importance that principles have in the founding of any co-operative enterprise. Although principles have their original roots in idealism, only those that work in reality can have any chance of success. To create a new co-operative in Western Canada one could draw on three distinct sources: the liberal democratic, the nonliberal democratic, and the regional.

The first source is the principles that operate in existing co-ops in Canada. Since the dominant tradition is liberal democratic the Rochdale rules form a base for any new co-op. Not only are these principles widespread and well-known, but they are also recognized in legislation and have a proven track record in economic development. Rochdale rules would give the new co-op a starting point that is credible. A second source of practical principles are those found in the other successful co-operative traditions, which may be relevant to the Canadian situation. The third source are principles that arise from the social history of the region.

The first group of principles is the Rochdale rules. Of these the principle of voluntary membership is fundamental. Free and voluntary association is the only acceptable form of grouping compatible with Canadian liberal democratic society. The kind of party-initiated and state-directed collectives found in communist countries is inappropriate and impossible in countries that have not undergone a Marxist revolution.

123

The second Rochdale principle is democracy. Any new co-operative must be operated democratically on a one-person/one-vote basis. This is a Canadian tradition that is also common to other political economies. Associated with democractic control is open membership which means that the co-operative, when seeking new members, must consider anyone who agrees with the objects of the co-op and can contribute to its well-being and advancement. This means the co-op must be non-partisan and nondenominational. In short, the co-op is a secular organization. But this openness does not mean that members do not have political or religious views. Rather it means that members do not have to subscribe to any particular party or denomination to be eligible for membership. The remaining principles of limited return on capital, education of members in co-operative philosophy, and co-operation among co-operatives must also be part of any new co-op.

But once this new co-op has adopted the principles of the Rochdale model, it cannot stop there or else it would simple be a reincarnation of a liberal democratic co-op. It has to turn to the other traditions for its second set of principles. From these other traditions come principles that can respond to both the general socio-economic problems of the region and the issues facing liberal democratic co-ops in Canada.

The first and most important of these nonliberal democratic principles is egalitarianism. Because of their opposition to private property, the Marxist, socialist and communalist traditions encourage egalitarianism and hold it up as one of the fundamental goals of the co-operative structures they have established. Egalitarianism can contribute to eliminating income and other differences between people by limiting private property. As well, it can substantially reduce class exploitation and move a co-operative to a single uniform standard of living for all its members. Egalitarianism is a basic antidote to the economic and social hierarchy found in capitalist societies such as Canada's and it promotes grassroots control against bureaucratization and elitism. It means a commitment to equality in every aspect of one's life, a commitment liberal democratic co-ops lack.

The second of these principles is nationalism. The liberal democratic co-op is an international model that can be applied everywhere, but this new co-op would be region-oriented because the nationalism of Western Canada is regionalism. The new co-op would come from the people of the region, would be situated in the region, and would be committed to the region's economic development. With this orientation the new co-op would develop a structure suited to the West's historic need for industrialization and diversification. This regional focus would simply be a continuation of the Canadian tradition of co-operative development based in the regions.

The third principle is class-consciousness. Although class-awareness is not officially part of today's Canadian co-ops, it certainly played a role in the utopian and movement phases of various kinds of co-ops in this country. Since co-operatives in their ideological stage are strongly anti-capitalist and populist in orientation, any new co-op would share this characteristic. It would be oriented to the needs of the majority—the working class. The co-op would be open to anyone, whatever his or her class background, who accepts the co-op's working class nature and goals.

The fourth principle is evolutionary development. In this it would not view itself as part of a revolutionary political process, such as that in which Marxist collectives participate. The basic commitment of the co-op would be to compete with capitalism and to survive economically in the marketplace as do liberal democratic co-ops. Evolutionary development is a commitment to peaceful social change, which is the basis of both the socialist and communalist traditions. In these traditions, co-operation is an island of egalitarianism in a sea of capitalism. The socialism of the new co-op would consist of a noncapitalist system of democratic and equitable self-management and ownership rather than socialism as a system of state ownership. Its socialism would advance social rather than public ownership of the means of production through self-governing co-operatives. To attempt to give this new co-op the goal of replacing or removing capitalism in Canada would be foolhardy and impractical. Neither the liberal democratic, nor the socialist, nor the communalist traditions that operate in capitalist societies have achieved this and there is no reason to expect a new co-op to be able to accomplish what those traditions have not been able to do previously.

The fifth principle is decentralization. This principle is most advanced in the communalist tradition, especially the religious one, which encourages a high degree of autonomy and self-direction. But decentralization is also found in the Marxist tradition in Yugoslav self-management and within the socialist tradition in kibbutzim. A commitment in the new co-op to decentralization would be an appropriate and necessary alternative to the kind of co-operative structures liberal democratic co-ops have established in their systems phase. Decentralization would allow grassroots and popular energy to emerge and play a determining role. It would encourage variety and constructive competition and it would maintain smaller units of co-operation, where ideals and ideology are powerful.

The sixth principle is multifunctionalism. This is the approach found in the nonliberal democratic co-ops, where co-operation exists in many areas and the co-operative structure provides a variety of services under one corporate umbrella. Multifunctionalism would be a new development for Canadian co-operation and would require an initial extrapolation of selected features of the Marxist, socialist, and communalist traditions and their blending in an appropriate form for Western Canada. Multifunctionalism would mean that social issues like lack of community in large urban centres, the shrinking range of social welfare programs and increasing impoverishment of public sector services like education and health, the plight of the single parent family and continued high levels of unemployment would be dealt with through a single co-op structure such as found in the Israeli kibbutz, the Hutterite colony, or the Chinese commune.

With these six principles that are external to the dominant tradition in Canada, this new co-op would differ substantially from the co-ops that presently operate in Canada. But since they would also operate with commonly accepted Rochdale rules, the new co-ops would have a substantial element of familiarity. In fact, the hallmark of these co-ops would be the delicate balance they would maintain between the old and the new. They would be conservative in that they acknowledge and incorporate what is and they would be radical in that they seek to realize new values. In this way they would be both part of the historical tradition and an advancement of it.

The third set of principles that these new co-ops would incorporate comes from contemporary socio-economic needs that are specific to the region. The first of these principles is social action or solidarity. Considering the serious disruption that the region is undergoing during the Eighties, it would be a basic requirement of this new co-op that its members commit themselves to solidarity work outside the co-op. Already, liberal democratic co-ops have begun to institute a "social audit" in which they assess on an annual basis their performance in the social and cultural needs of the area in which they are situated. A new co-op would take this further by instituting social programs in the areas of health, education, and social aid, which members would carry out as part of their membership responsibilities.

The second of these local principles is self-reliance. Considering the dependent nature of the region's economy on foreign markets and foreign capital, the encouragement of a pioneering spirit of self-reliant resourcefulness and independence would be an effective counter to the uncommitted attitude of most liberal democratic co-op members. Self-help has always been a cornerstone of co-operation. Self-help generates an atmosphere of mutual commitment and responsibility. Within this context strong fraternal and community ties can develop.

The third local principle is the open principle. It is important that the principles listed above not be exhaustive or all-inclusive, so that a space is left open into which the members can put their own principle. For example, one of these new co-ops might wish to display an ecological commitment, while another might wish to be pacifist in its goals. The freedom to select and implement a principle of their own choosing is vital to the strength and growth of these co-operatives. People who are fundamentally involved in a particular issue would be able to seek out this co-op as one way of living what they preach.

When we combine the half-dozen Rochdale rules with the six external principles and the three local principles, we have fifteen basic principles to which this new co-op would be committed. That may seem like a lot, but the principles complement and reinforce each other and they weave a strong web by which human relations in the co-op are determined. As with all principles, these are open to interpretation when they are implemented. In theory they sound simple and clear enough but when put into practice by human beings they will no doubt be implemented with a certain amount of contradiction, compromise, and experimentation. Only in that way will they become capable of realization.

THE FIFTEEN PRINCIPLES OF SOCIAL CO-OPERATIVES
1. The liberal democratic principles:
   voluntary membership
   democratic control
   secular organization
   limited return on capital
   education of members in co-operative philosophy
   co-operation among co-operatives
2. The nonliberal democratic principles:
   egalitarianism
   nationalism
   class-consciousness
   evolutionary development
   decentralization
   multifunctionalism
3. The regional principles:
   solidarity
   self-reliance
   open principle
   To get a sense of how these principles might operate in practice, one

can begin by showing how they are a reflection of what is already happening in the other traditions. In short, how would this new co-op either be based on or identify with such co-operative forms as that of Mondragon or a Chinese commune or a kibbutz?

THE NEW CO-OPERATIVE AND THE HISTORICAL TRADITION

The historical tradition of co-operation, divided into its four component parts—liberal democratic, Marxist, socialist, and communalist, is composed of failure and success. It is important for any new co-operative to build on the successful models rather than on those that were short-lived or economically deficient. Since this new co-op would seek to advance the general cause of co-operation, it would have to find its predecessors among those models which advanced co-operation.

Since this new co-op would be based in part on the Rochdale rules, it would have to relate to the dominant tradition in Canada. No matter what elements the new co-op may adopt from foreign models, it would always have to reinterpret them in such a way as to blend with liberal democratic precedence.

There are three main points of contact between the new co-op and the Canadian situation. First, this new co-op would recognize the regional character and regional origins of Canadian co-operation by adopting a regional focus for its work. This Western Canadian orientation would be akin to the history of the *caisse populaire* movement in Quebec or the Antigonish Movement in the Maritimes. Second, this new co-op would recognize the diversity of areas of operation in which liberal democratic co-ops are presently engaged. It would make consumption, production, housing, and industry vital to its mandate. It would seek to provide all the services that liberal democratic co-ops now provide but in a single, multifunctional entity. So a person joining the new co-op would find a familiar reality organized in a novel way.

This combination of identity and difference is important because it shows how the new co-op is rooted in the familiar and the established, while at the same time pointing to a new reality. A person joining the new co-op would find the liberal democratic tradition alive and well within a nonliberal democratic structure.

Third, the new co-op would need to make every effort to relate positively and constructively to the social sector, represented in the main by Canadian co-operatives. There are several reasons for this requirement. First, the new co-op would be a result of the self-criticism initiated by liberal democratic co-ops and so it should be considered a product of that critique. It would be an attempt to answer the problems associated with their systems phase. As well, the new co-op would view itself as a partner in the broad historical tradition and so is linked to the liberal democratic co-ops through a heritage of shared values and principles. Because this new co-op would not be a liberal democratic one, it would balance the kind of co-ops existing in Canada. Although the new co-op would be reliant on its own resources and strategy of development, it would also need the support of the Canadian cooperative movement if it is to flourish. John Jordan pointed to this need when he made the following observations about the emerging worker co-op movement in Canada in the 1980s:

> Without a commitment, and an energetic one, by the co-operative sector, it is extremely unlikely that worker co-operatives will assume significant proportions in Canada.[2]

The decade of the 1970s showed how true this was of Canada. During that decade two new kinds of liberal democratic co-ops appeared: consumer health food co-ops and housing co-ops. The former had great difficulty relating to the existing consumer co-ops, which was a loss to both sides.[3] The health food co-ops survived tenuously because there was no mutual support, while the established retail food co-ops missed out on this important trend in nutrition. In contrast, the housing co-ops did very well. In the space of 15 years and with the help of state funds, they created a membership of 103,000. They have been able to maintain strong democratic control and high member involvement because each of the incorporated housing co-ops is small. Yet they have national clout through their membership in the Co-operative Union of Canada.

Since this new co-op would not be a liberal democratic one, it would most likely face stiffer opposition from the established system than either the health food or housing co-ops did. Yet the established system's interest in worker co-ops complements a similar interest of the new co-op and is a point of mutual contact.

If the liberal democratic tradition is so important what would the Marxist tradition have to offer a new co-op in Western Canada? To answer that question one would have to divide the three components of the Marxist tradition—Russian, Chinese, and Yugoslavian—along the success/failure grid. Of the three, the Russian kolkhoz is more of a failure than the Chinese commune and workers' self-management.

The decision to consider the Russian kolkhoz a co-operative failure is based on its poor economic performance and its tendency to be supplanted by the state farm. The kolkhoz has been the least productive and least democratic of communist co-operative organizations. The commune and workers' self-management have been more successful in meeting the goals set for them by the political leadership of their respective countries and have come closer to their ideals. The other main difficulty with using the kolkhoz as a model is that it is purely agricultural, while the main focus of the new Western Canadian co-op is industrial.

The first point of contact between the new co-op and the Chinese commune is its forerunner—the Indusco movement of World War II. Like the new co-op Indusco had industrial goals. The decentralized and small-size orientation of the new co-op would fit with the Chinese commune model, which rejected the Soviet strategy of centralized, large-scale industry. The Chinese communes were also an attempt at integrating industrial and agricultural functions into semi-sufficient communities. This Maoist attack on specialization and experts has been criticized for fostering inefficiency and technical backwardness. But it is not so much the theory of decentralized production that caused problems as the communist tendency to force implementation in an extremely short period. It is the impossible time schedules that produce vast economic disruptions. And finally, the multifunctional nature of the new co-op would fit well with the nature of the Chinese commune, which was meant to provide a wide range of services.

The value of the Yugoslavian experience is its focus on workers and self-management in the workplace. The system encourages interfirm competition under the concept of "market socialism" which can be one way of viewing economic relations in a co-operative commonwealth where social production is the norm. Like the Chinese, the Yugoslav model encourages decentralization and it exemplifies the development of an indigenous interpretation of Marxism.

What is relevant in the Chinese and the Yugoslav models is the use of predominantly co-operative rather than state ownership models to develop agricultural economies and to industrialize. Both countries have succeeded in transforming their economies through self-reliance and popular mobilization via co-operative organs. For a region like Western Canada which has always sought to escape primary production and to have its own economic development, the Chinese and Yugoslav experience is valuable.

In the post-Mao period, which has witnessed a move away from Mao's communal strategy, there are developments that link China and Yugoslavia. China has been developing a new nonstate, noncapitalist sector, which operates within a market socialism concept like Yugoslavia's. The emphasis is on socially responsible nonstate ownership of certain industries. A *Globe and Mail* article on this "semi-private" sector pointed out that most of the shareholders in a former state-owned firm are employees, and they are allowed to move shares only among themselves.[4] This sector is meant to stimulate a moribund public sector.

What limits the relevance of the Marxist tradition to the new co-op is its revolutionary heritage. Since the new co-op is committed to evolution within capitalism, it has more in common with the socialist tradition than the Marxist one. And of the three socialist models— Mondragon, kibbutz, and ujamaa village—Mondragon and the kibbutz are the more relevant. Like the kolkhoz the ujamaa village is an agricultural model and its poor economic performance limits its relevance to the new co-op.

At Mondragon there are a large number of factors which do relate to the new co-op. Of these the most important is the worker co-operative base that gives substance to all the activities at Mondragon. The prime goal of employment in a region with a chronic unemployment problem fits a major goal of this new co-op. The geographic limits that Mondragon has placed on its activities would be similar to the new co-op's need to focus on Western Canada.

But it is the way the worker co-ops at Mondragon operate that relates best to the new co-op. The lack of hired labour, the emphasis on income equality and employment security, the importance of co-operative education from daycare to university, and the requirement of a large capital stake for each member makes Mondragon very different from the liberal democratic tradition, where membership may cost as little as one dollar.

Mondragon's comprehensive social security package, which is self-administered, is a model for those places where public programs are insufficient or of deteriorating quality. Since this is a factor in Canada, Mondragon is important. The financial system at Mondragon is also an indicator of what capital requirements for industrial co-ops might be and how those capital needs can be met by drawing on the savings of the region's population.

But ultimately it is the community aspects of Mondragon that are impressive. In Spain there are many individual worker co-ops but only at Mondragon is there an integrated community structure based on the Basque identity. Since this new Western Canadian co-op would aim at becoming a co-operative community, Mondragon has a great deal to teach it about the evolution of a community structure rooted in worker co-ops.

The successful socialism of Mondragon is matched by the successful socialism of the kibbutzim. The prime contribution of the kibbutzim is the way in which they blended nationalist and socialist objectives,

131

especially in the pre-independence period. This ability to marry Zionism with socialism and thereby generate an indigenous ideology rooted in both Jewish history and European radicalism is certainly relevant to the impulse underlying the new co-op, which is based on a joint commitment to the region and to workers.

Secondly, strict egalitarianism in consumption and production is a hallmark of the kibbutz and one which sets a high standard for the new co-op to attempt to emulate. The kibbutz has created a system of equality (outside of hired labour) that integrates the individual into a community which in turn is integrated into a larger national project. Mondragon has yet to achieve such a high degree of equality and political integration.

Although the kibbutz began as an agricultural farm settlement project, its present agro-industrial nature is a good example of flexibility and economic momentum. Perhaps the new Western Canadian co-op would reverse the farm to factory direction because we do not have the same Zionist settler imperative here. The natural movement here would be factory-to-farm and the creation of an industrial agrarian-community.

Finally, the kibbutz would teach the new co-op how vital is the need for supporting institutions to subsidize a social movement. Without the donations of various organizations to the kibbutz, the kibbutz would never have achieved the stature which it did.

Mondragon and the kibbutz have set a numerical standard by which this new co-op, as a secular movement, could be judged to have reached a world-class level. Mondragon, after thirty years, embraces about 4 percent of the Basque region's population, while the kibbutzim contain about 3 percent of the Jewish population of Israel. If we take the present population of the three prairie provinces (4.5 million) and project it twenty-five years into the future, a figure of 100,00 to 200,000 members would be needed to make it a world-class co-operative community.

These figures far surpass the numbers involved in the communalist tradition, yet that tradition would be extremely important to the new co-op because it is so well established in the region. Of the two parts of the communalist tradition—religious and political—it is the religious one that is more successful. Western Canada has been fortunate in possessing the world's most successful religious commune, the Hutterites, and this fact should provide the new co-op with an impetus to examine the Hutterite heritage.

Of the failures in communalism, the nineteenth century utopians and the counterculture movement of the twentieth century have the least to offer the new co-op. Their brevity and American origins are not conducive to the long-range regional goals of the new co-op. But the co-op farm movement in Western Canada would have a great deal to teach the new co-op about the difficulties facing new social movements.

The Hutterites offer several useful organizationl aspects that could be incorporated into the new co-op in spite of the Hutterites religious and agricultural lifestyle. First, their emphasis on small-size communities (around 100 people including children) is an excellent way in which to preserve direct democracy. This size also makes possible "the conditions of social predictability" which allow social incentives and community pressure to be most effective.[5] Second, their family orientation is much better suited to a secular community than the monastic, celibate model. Third, their practice of the community of goods and the intensity of their communal sharing creates a superior degree of egalitarianism. Fourth, the Hutterites have pioneered a variety of legal and economic relations with the governments of Western Canada which create a precedent that may be useful in meeting the new co-op's legislative needs.

Unfortunately, there are factors that limit the appropriateness of Hutterite model. Its religious orientation, its agricultural lifestyle and emphasis on anachronistic clothing would all be inappropriate in the new co-op. The Hutterite retreat from society would be the opposite of the new co-op's social orientation.

Monastic communalism does have a few aspects that could be useful to the new co-op. The requirement of a probationary period for new members is important. The balance between manual and intellectual labour is also helpful to the liberation of the individual, as is the sense of peacefulness found in monastic life.

The blending of aspects from each of the four co-operative traditions would make the new co-op unique. It would not be a clone of any one of the models found in four traditions, but it would be open to each of them. By drawing on precedents it would pick and choose what is best suited to the region and then test those features through trial and error.

SOCIAL RELATIONS IN THE NEW CO-OP

The ideology of the new co-operative would encompass the role of the individual, the role of the family, the community life of the co-op, and relations with society. The new co-op would create relations within itself so that no person could use his or her wealth to exploit others. Julius Nyerere called this 'socialism'—a system committed to "the well-being of the people."[6]

What the individual would find in the new co-operative would be

133

severe restrictions on private property matched by a strong emphasis on social ownership, production-oriented values, and a work ethic. In return for the individual's labour and constructive participation, the co-operative would guarantee three things: an equal voice in determining the affairs of the co-op; community responsibility for each member's welfare based on the principle of "unqualified mutual liability"[7]; and an environment operating on clear, previously enunciated principles secured by organizational commitments to the individual of a constitutional and contractual nature.

Henrik Infield, the twentieth century sociologist of co-operative communities, wrote in *Utopia and Experiment* that "the motive power in all human activity is need."[8] It is the needs that the new co-op would satisfy that would be paramount in attracting certain individuals and families to the co-op. Since the focus of the co-op would be employment, it would be natural that the unemployed would want to examine the co-op as an employment option. And of those suffering from unemployment, it is the youth who suffer the most. Recent figures show that in Canada, male youths between the ages of 15 and 24 have twice the unemployment rate of mature workers.[9]

At the other end of the age spectrum are retired people. They would benefit from the stimulation of an multigenerational community and by the sense of security, caring, and belonging which they would find in the co-op. Leah Cohen in her recent book, *Small Expectations: Society's Betrayal of Older Women*, describes the social conditions of poverty and neglect faced by the majority of single, older women in Canadian society.[10] Their need for autonomy mixed with social involvement goes far beyond what contemporary nursing homes offer. And as the number of aging citizens grows, so does the need to incorporate them into community life.

Between young adults and retired people lies the bulk of the productive society and for this group the major emphasis is on the family and the problems families face today. Statistical information indicates that traditional family patterns have altered radically in the past fifteen years. Soon 15 percent of Canada's six million families will be single parent lead—that means almost one million families.[11] Eighty percent of these single parents are women and they face a serious drop in income after separation or divorce, a shortage of daycare facilities, and the emotional stress of juggling parenting and careers. In today's society single parents lack options and ongoing support. The new co-op would provide that supporting and nurturing environment which would enable single parent families to survive.

An emphasis on the family in the co-op would mean the creation of a social environment that would allow all spouses to work. In the majority of marriages that is already the case.[12] Yet employers expect employees to give priority to work instead of the family. The co-op would reverse this by providing the social relationships and economic structures that would allow family life to become a focal point. Because of the co-op's commitment to equality and equal pay there would be no monopolies for either sex in any sphere. The co-op would encourage equal marriages in which tasks, responsibilities and privileges are shared.

The physical space that corresponds to this social vision is not the typical single-family suburban home. Group housing is an increasingly common form of shelter in North American society and more and more family meals are taken outside the home. Dolores Hayden's recent statement that society needs to encourage housing that meets "the special needs of the elderly, single parents, battered wives and single people" would fit the co-op's vision.[13] She calls for a strategy of neighborhoods that create nurturing and paid work in one space, provide housing and collective services, and promote economic development. The new co-op would provide just such a strategy as it builds a multifunctional, multifamily environment.

The emphasis on the family within an egalitarian community is comparable to the emphasis found in both the kibbutz and the Hutterite colony. It also exists in all co-ops from the ujamaa village to the Chinese commune. Menachem Gerson has written that "stability in the family is a prime way of ensuring kibbutz life."[14] Yet the family in the kibbutz is not an economic unit in competition with other families. It is the co-operative as a whole that is the economic unit to which members contribute and whose health determines the well-being of the family.

Community is the intermediate stage between individuals and families on the one hand and society on the other. It is community that mediates between the personal closeness of the family and the obligations of society. The American philosopher Baker Brownell claims that it is within community that values are created which dignify living and that commitment to community is necessary for a healthy society.[15] Community creates the context in which certain individual values and family practices are encouraged and validated. If the new co-op did not have a community structure it would be deprived of a valuable social structure.

The question of what constitutes community is a wide-ranging philosophical and sociological issue. Suffice it to say that the German term 'Gemeinde' comes closest to what I mean. The Gemeinde is a small local community, the French equivalent of which is *la communauté.*[16]

The new co-op would attempt to create a *Gemeinde* as described by the philosopher Martin Buber:

> the need of man to feel that his own house is part of some greater, all-embracing structure in which he is at home, the need to feel that others with whom he lives and works all acknowledge and confirm...an association based on community of views and aspirations...[17]

To create the reality of a Gemeinde requires the kind of proximity in which face to face human relations are possible and where a sense of belonging is well-developed. Brownell makes the point that in the community, as opposed to mass society, the range and content of a man's identification with the group has an "organic solidarity" through all the phases of a person's life.[18]

Of the four co-operative traditions, the communal one is the most concerned with community life. Both religious and political writers have commented on the importance of community life in maintaining communal values. Sister Marce Beha sees the intentional human community, as distinct from the inherited ones into which we are born as the embodiment of a certain spirit or values.[19] Joseph Blasi, the contemporary American expert on the kibbutz, claims that the kibbutz is just the kind of structure that those who opt for "co-operation as a way of life" would create.[20]

The nature of community life within the new co-op would be developed by the members' practical response to the principle of community. Blasi offers the following advice:

> The intention for fellowship and the energy to visualize and create social alternatives must be deeply felt and must have a persistent significance for the individuals who try to create local community within a larger society. The substance of this intention and the plan for an alternative cannot be copied. The central point is that such a plan must direct the citizen-pioneers energy effectively and must take into account wisely the possibilities existing in the present environment.[21]

The "present environment" to which Blasi refers is not just the socio-economic structure but the cultural milieu out of which the co-op's members come and within which the co-op must thrive. That cultural milieu includes the mores, the unspoken understandings and the acceptable practices of the day. The following vision of the ujamaa villages presented by Julius Nyerere twenty years ago captures the spirit of his time and his place and the mood of the Tanzanian people in their moment of self-determination.

> In a socialist Tanzania then, our agricultural organization would be predominantly that of co-operative living and working for the good of all. This means that most of our farming would be done by groups of people who live as a community and work as a community. They would live together; market together; and undertake the provision of local services and small local requirements as a community. Their community would be the traditional family group or any other group of people living according to ujamaa principles...The land this community farms would be called "our land" by all the members; the crops they produced on that land would be "our crop"; it would be "our shop" which provided individual members with the day to day necessities from outside...and so on.[22]

The following statement by a Canadian is a much better reflection of the contemporary situation in our country.

> It is not uncommon lately in some centres to find a household which lives in a housing co-op, buys its groceries at a food co-op, does its banking at a credit union and sends its children to co-op day care.[23]

In defining community life in the new co-op this latter statement has more relevance to our time and place than does Nyerere's in spite of its eloquence.

The new co-operative would have to relate to society and that relationship would have to be based on an ongoing identification with the needs of society and its social and political evolution. Unlike communes, the new co-op would not be a withdrawal or an escape. But the co-op's one-way identification with society would not be enough. It would also require society's acceptance of the new co-op and such acceptance would be dependent on the image that it has for society.

The new co-op's commitment to Western Canadian economic development would be fundamental to achieving mutual identification between community and society. Likewise the co-op's commitment to egalitarian and co-operative values would appeal to certain segments of society, especially if the co-op is successful in improving conditions for women, the unemployed, and single-parent families. Both Mondragon and kibbutz history show us that national support is crucial for both attracting members and ensuring a place for the institution in society. In Western Canada the most that the new co-op could hope for is the kind of general acceptance accorded liberal democratic co-ops and the least that it would require is the reluctant tolerance given the Hutterites.

By striving to eliminate alienation between itself and society, and itself and the wider co-operative movement, the new co-op would ensure its own survival and growth, but, more important, it would offer renewal to both the co-operative movement and Western Canadian society.

Chapter Eight:
THE PRACTICE

FROM WORKER CO-OP TO CO-OPERATIVE COMMUNITY

To express its identity, the new co-operative requires a name. But since it would be a hybrid of the four traditions, naming presents a problem. In Chapter Six the point was made that the word 'co-operative' when used as a noun rightly belongs to the liberal democratic tradition and when used as an adjective it belongs to the socialist tradition, that the correct term for the Marxist co-ops is 'collective' and for the communalist ones 'commune.' This neat division is not all that helpful when a co-op mixes and blends elements from all the traditions. To describe this kind of co-operative requires creativity and compromise.

On the one hand the new co-op is a series of Rochdale co-ops, which means it is entitled to used the word 'co-operative' as a noun, while on the other hand, as a community, it would have the right to use 'co-operative' as an adjective. The term 'social co-operative' is one that expresses both these uses. It is not perfect but it does the job.

Since the tradition in Canada is liberal democratic, co-operative communities would be a new element. The more they can be identified with the usage and practice of the liberal democratic co-ops the easier they will be to accept. Canadians are already aware of consumer co-ops, producer co-ops. and housing co-ops to which can be added 'social co-ops.' The word "social" refers to the self-contained community that is the co-op and its mandate to relate to the wider society.

It would be useful to have a term in English such as 'kolkhoz', or 'ujamaa' or 'ashram' to describe the new co-op, but such a term does not exist and so the indigenous quality that the foreign terms give their co-ops is not available to the new co-op.

The motto of the social co-ops can be summarized as "working together, living together, owning together." Through a united system of worker co-ops, housing co-ops, daycare and school co-ops, the social co-op would build a kind of community found in the socialist tradition of other countries.

The motto of the social co-ops expresses the priorities of the community. First and foremost is "working together." Working together refers to worker co-ops. They would be the starting point for any social co-op and its heart. The worker co-ops would be small because the social co-op would be small. Worker co-ops would employ the adult members and ensure that the means of production are the collective property of the co-op. A single social co-op would have several worker co-ops. It in turn would belong to a wider body of social co-ops. So the control of the enterprises would rest in a combination of workers in the enterprise, the social co-op to which it belongs, and the movement to which the co-operative community is affiliated.

Working together means more than worker co-ops; it means practices within the worker co-ops themselves. In the first instance it means that membership in a social co-op entitles one to work in that co-op's industries. Of course, there would be a period of transition for new members, who will need time to move from their previous occupations into new ones. As well, the social co-op in its start-up stage may need outside employment to supplement its income. But there would have to be a time limit for outside employment.

Another aspect of working together is self-labour. That means that only co-op members could work in co-op industries. There would be no hired help as found in the kibbutz. Adherence to self-labour would be stretched to include probationary members and volunteers. Through self-labour the co-op can avoid an internal class system and the labour problems that beset liberal democratic co-ops. Of course, this means that expansion of production is dependent on member recruitment and/or labour-saving technology, both of which would improve the co-op.

And finally, working together means equal pay for all members. There can be no wage differences in the social co-op because the work of the child care worker is equal to the work of the manager or the work of the cook. It should be noted that the definition of work includes solidarity work that would be part of every member's duty.

To summarize: working together means organizing work into worker co-operatives; it means that physically and mentally able members must work in the co-op industries; it means no hired labour; it means equal pay; and it means participation in the solidarity projects of the co-op.

"Living together" is the second part of the motto and refers to the social aspects of community life. It would follow on the establishment

140

of worker co-ops and would involve shelter, food, clothing, and ancillary services such as childcare, education, and medical care. Shelter would be provided in the form of a liberal democratic housing co-op just as employment was provided in the form of a liberal democractic worker co-op. The housing co-op would offer a sense of proximity and neighbourhood while ensuring individual privacy, family grouping, and communal facilities. In order to preserve the unity of the social co-op it would be best to have only one housing co-op per social co-op.

Besides the housing co-op, living together would involve some form of communal eating. In the kibbutz and the Hutterite colony all meals are taken communally. This is suited to an agricultural milieu but it would be more difficult to achieve in an urban setting unless the homes of the members were next to their places of work or in the vicinity. Perhaps a social co-op could achieve this standard but a minimum requirement would be one community meal per week.

The third aspect is clothing. In religous communes distinctive clothing is used to separate the members from the outside world. The monk has the religious habit of his order; the Hutterites have their distinctive religious costume; and followers of the Indian guru, Rasjneesh, wear orange at his ashram-ranch in Oregon. Since the social co-op would be a secular community, distinctive dress is unnecessary.

The final aspect of living together is the ancillary social services like education and health care that the co-op would provide. In order to develop a strong sense of mutual responsibility and to pass on the values of co-operation to the next generation, the social co-op would require its own daycare, and educational programs. The nature of these services and how they would be paid for and at what point they would become essential can only be determined as the needs of the community and its ability to provide for them expands.

But it is the final part of the motto "owning together" that pushes co-operation to a new plateau. Owning together is the cement that binds the social co-op together and sets it apart from the private-property oriented society in which it exists. In the social co-op, co-operative ownership would be predominant and egalitarian sharing the ideal. The following hypothetical case is an example of how owning together might operate.

A husband and wife with two children decide to join a social co-op. The first financial commitment they will face is investment in a share/loan of the co-op. The cost of this share/loan would be high, with Mondragon standards setting the norm. Let us say it is $5,000 per adult in 1985 dollars and $2,500 per child. The family would then have to pay out $15,000 to join. Compare this with $5 of share capital in a credit union or $500 in a housing co-op. It is substantial and is meant to test the seriousness of the member and to provide the co-op with capital and operating funds. This money would earn only limited interest under Rochdale rules and it would be the only thing other than personal effects that the member could bring into the co-op and take out again.

Making the cost of entrance the same for all ensures equality within the co-op and precludes those with greater funds from exerting greater influence. Supposing the family that joined the co-op, after paying its capital share, still had substantial assets left over. These assets would have to be put in trust and could not be used by the member while in the co-op. Should the member leave then he would re-acquire use of these funds. The member would also have the option of using a privately controlled trust or the co-op's own trust, which would invest in co-op industries. The only way in which outside assets could be transfered to the co-op would through the willing of these assets upon the death of the member.

Limiting access to private outside assets would also be reflected in the co-op's practice of taking all the outside salary earnings of members who may be temporarily working outside the co-op's industries. The income would go into the common pot. The basic approach is that assets held prior to membership remain the private property of the member but cannot be used by the member while in the co-op. Whatever income comes from outside once the person is a member goes to the community. For example, should a member receive an inheritance that money becomes the co-op's property. If the member does not wish this to happen he or she can leave and take the money with them.

What about the unemployed and the working poor who have few assets and cannot pay the cost of a share? Mondragon shows how this cost can be deducted from a worker's salary until the share is paid for. Initially social co-ops could not afford to do this but in time they could provide such loans to prospective members. In the beginning, an outside fund would have to be established to provide this money. The fund would draw on donations from outside the co-op.

Owning together means that each member has only one share and one vote and that his ownership exists only as long as he or she is a member. Ownership ends with the termination of membership. But ownership cannot involve individual profit. In other words, members of a co-op cannot decide to wind up the affairs of the co-op, sell the assets, and distribute the proceeds amongst themselves. Should a social co-op wind up then the proceeds remaining after the share holders and debts are paid off are returned to a central co-ordinating body to which the social co-op is affiliated and from which its charter comes. These repatriated funds would then be used to fund existing social co-ops or launch new ones. This practice is basic to the view that as long as one is in the co-op one has access to all the co-op can provide, but one can never use the co-op for one's private profit.

David Wright in *Co-operatives and Community: The Theory and Practice of Producer Co-operatives* confirms this approach when he explains how the three elements of ownership—the right of control, the right of benefit, and the right of transfer—ought to work in co-operatives. He says that co-operative control means worker control, that the benefit of ownership must accrue to the members as long as the co-op exists, and that the right of transfer means the right of transfer only to other co-operatives.[1] Owning together is the most complex and difficult of the three 'togethers' but when achieved it is the most satisfying of the three.

FROM CO-OPERATIVE COMMUNITY TO SOCIAL MOVEMENT

A number of years ago Charles Gide wrote that "lay communities," in contrast to religious ones, had such a poor survival record because of quarrels between individuals and families, difficulty in submitting to discipline and difficulty in stifling the sense of ownership and individual gain.[2] Lacking that overall and supreme religious sanction, secular communities have found it difficult to sustain themselves. This fact became evident in the survey of political communes in Chapter Five. For this reason it must be made clear that a social co-operative is not a commune. It is a system of integrated co-operative entities creating a co-operative community similar to those found in the socialist tradition.

The interpersonal problems and the antagonisms generated by established habits can become overwhelming when the organizational and institutional structure is a communal one that is isolated, small, and alienated from society. In this situation the difficulties Gide mentioned can become issues of paramount importance, and so it is incumbent on the social co-ops to organize themselves in such a manner that these problems are kept in check. There are five areas that need careful planning to prevent the breakdown of the co-operative community: people, money, the law, taxation, and expansion.

Social co-ops can only thrive when the members have the skills, ideology and commitment to make the co-ops work. George Davidovic stressed the primary importance of people to co-operation when he wrote:

> The building of the co-operative economy depends primarily on people, on co-opeartive members; it depends on their activity, their

zeal, their devotion to the co-operative cause, their involvement in co-operative affairs, their resoluteness and perseverance. A co-operative can succeed, progress, and prosper only if the people who are its members need it, support it, establish close and continuous relationship with it, care for it, control it.[3]

Since the centre of each social co-op is a worker co-op or co-ops those who could contribute to these industries would be the most sought after members. The goal of Western Canadian industrialization means that the co-ops would require engineers and other professionals to create products and market goods. The co-op would need educated members able to operate in a technologically-advanced environment. The graduate engineers who founded Mondragon are one model, as are the founders of the kibbutzim. Dr. Darin-Drabkin noted the comments of many observers on the high intellectual standards of kibbutz members. He says that the reason for this is that the founders of the kibbutz came from "middle-class" families. He gives a 1926 statistic showing that 50 percent of Jewish immigrants to Palestine had either a secondary school or university education and that those who chose agricultural work had an even higher percentage.[4]

What this indicates is that the utopian phase of co-operation and the skills necessary to make it work need a significant level of achievement among its members. Jaroslav Vanek, a leading authority on self-management in the Yugoslav model, wrote recently that for self-management to work in North America there must be strong motivation, a high level of consciousness, and a comprehension of the problems involved.[5] Unfortunately none of these elements is encouraged in capitalist society. For this reason social co-ops will need a period of education and probation for new members during which time the member and the group can evaluate each other.

Next to people, the most important matter is financing or capital. Unless the co-op has sufficient funds to develop its industries and to provide the services it must, it will not survive. The capital needs of a social co-op are substantial and the methods of raising large sums will be varied. At Mondragon 20 percent of the capital comes from worker-owners; 20 percent comes from a special government fund; and 60 percent comes from the Caja Laboral, Mondragon's bank. Using this formula as a guide, it is clear that the share or loan capital of members, although very high by liberal democratic standards, would only be a minor part of what is needed.

In Canada there are several sources of funding. Governments at all levels provide grants, low-cost loans, and other incentives for businesses. The industries run by the co-op would be eligible for job-creation support and special worker co-op programs should they arise. Likewise, in the area of housing, both provincial and federal government programs exist to assist the building of inexpensive social housing, for which the housing co-ops could apply. But even with state subsidies, there would be need for substantial private funding.

At the beginning the major source of private funding would be something similar to the Jewish National Fund, which would attract donations from individuals and organizations wishing to support Western Canadian social development. The fund would be an organization with a broad mandate that would include the work of social co-ops.

But such a fund would probably be insufficient to finance a large social movement and so at some stage in their history, the social co-ops would have to create their own vehicle. And here the Mondragon example is so important. The Caja Laboral, the working people's bank, has been one of the cornerstone's of Mondragon's success and one that the social co-ops would want to emulate.

In Canada we have four kinds of financial institutions: banks, trust companies, credit unions, and assorted mortgage and finance companies. No doubt, the first social co-ops would create their own credit union to handle their members' funds but limited social co-op membership would result in small institutions to being with. The establishment of a trust company would allow the social co-ops to draw on deposits from the wider society and use those funds for sound investments in worker co-ops. And eventually social co-ops would need to have their own bank. Since Canada's banking laws are no longer as exclusive as they once were, this goal is not an impossible dream.

If the social co-ops are to attract the right people and sufficient capital to achieve their goals, they will have to deal with the limitations of present legislation on social property. Today's co-op law is based solely on the needs of liberal democratic co-operatives. The farm producer co-ops, the credit unions, and the retail stores have created a body of legislation which protects their interests. This legislation is only partially suited to the needs of co-operative communities. Initially, the social co-ops will have to adopt a strategy of accomodation with the existing legal system the way Mondragon did.[6] This does not preclude changes in legislation or the introduction of legislation specifically for social co-ops.

What social co-ops need in order to create favourable legislation is to establish their own internal constitutional framework that reflects their needs and values. Once this framework has been shown to work well, relevant parts of it can be incorporated in law. Of course, social

145

co-ops will need to have some presence in society before the state will deem it necessary to sanction them in legislation.

Taxation is the next area of importance after legislation. Canada's liberal democratic co-ops have faced an uneasy history of taxation since World War I. Since Canadian society is based on private property, social property has had difficulty in being recognized and treated as something different. In the case of communal ownership, only religious bodies have been able to get exemptions from taxation. Social co-ops will have to break new ground in order to preserve their values and practices.

One trend in taxation that is beneficial is the increasing dependence on personal income tax for government funds and a decreasing dependence on corporate taxation. Since the social co-op and its various components would be corporate entities it should be subject to corporate taxation rather than personal income taxes. This would aid the co-op because corporate taxes are lower than individual ones. It would also strengthen group identity.

These practical matters cannot be resolved in advance. They are part of the historical evolution of social co-ops and their role in Western Canadian society, but unless some serious thought is given to issues of labour, capital, legislation, and taxation prior to the establishment of social co-ops their chances of survival are lowered. It is in this planning stage that adjustments can be made to real conditions current in the country.

Planning to deal with the above problems culminates in the question of growth or expansion. The greatest tragedy that could befall social co-ops is that only one of them comes into being. The whole impetus of the social co-op idea is to create a network of co-operative communities rather than a single entity no matter how successful it may be. The institutional structure of co-ops, financial institutions, and funds is meaningless without a number of social co-ops being involved. Social co-ops must aim to be a social movement and not an isolated utopia. Moving in this direction means that social co-ops would seek to reflect the reality represented by the hundreds of kibbutzim, the hundred and twenty co-ops in the Mondragon group and the two hundred Hutterite colonies.

John Jordan has stated that "successful social movements extend beyond issuing a statement of ideology or a proclamation of a utopian vision: they mobilize and act. They establish organizations."[7] The essential point here is multiplicity. It is not only the multifunctionalism of the social co-op itself that is important; it is also the multiple nature of social co-ops and their unification in a single social movement that is vital. A historian of the kibbutzim, Harry Viteles, emphasizes that "no secular collectivist society has ever survived long as an isolated sectarian entity in a noncollectivist environment.''[8] For this reason alone, social co-ops must be a social movement and all that a social movement entails.

"The purpose of the movement process," writes Michel Chevalier, "is to develop a vision for co-operative development. It should concentrate on broad and integrated human needs and be holistic in focus...[and] sufficiently realistic to connect with the current situation.''[9] When the social co-ops view themselves as a social movement they will turn toward the creation of a unified network of communities that are mutually reinforcing. The strength provided by a social movement is basic to ensuring social co-op survival. It creates collective reserves necessary to weather inevitable crises and it articulates a body of shared principles and practices and encourages adherence to them.

When the various co-ops incorporated into a social co-op seek membership in liberal democratic federations, they would have their own system to return to. The organizations of the social movement will guide individual social co-ops, in the words of one expert on communal life, "to consciously build up a structure of social life and maintain it in explicit contrast to the structure of the larger society.''[10]

The three stages of co-operative development—utopian, movement, and system—are applicable to social co-ops. The utopian stage is the stage of initial establishment and survival. It would be reasonable to consider a decade as a kind of minimum time-span for this stage. During the utopian stage all the development and trial and error work would have to be done by the pioneers of the movement as they struggled to create viable forms. The movement stage would begin when the principles and practices of social co-ops had stabilized or were sufficiently institutionalized to have legislative sanction. The movement stage would have a generally acknowledged workable model ready to be adopted by new members. Finally the systems phase would appear when the social co-op movement had reached a certain maturity. In this phase would come the first calls for re-appraisal and renewal.

CONCLUSION

In this book I have attempted to clarify the history of co-operation through an examination of forms that exist outside the Canadian experience and I have tried to show how that multifaceted history relates to the development of a new co-operative in the region. But I do not suggest that I know the future of social co-ops. At this moment they are an idea. And like all ideas they await human beings to shape them.

Those who will build social co-operatives will take the original concept suggested here and mould it to suit their own originality. Their ideas, their needs, and their interpretations will interact with the limitations placed on their wishes by the environment in which they must operate. Out of this will come the first real social co-ops.

"We live today in a world where the need for constructive utopian vision is acute," writes Paula Rayman, the American author of *The Kibbutz Community and Nation-Building*, "a utopian vision indicates possibilities for a different mode of life, for different norms of interpersonal relations and of human organization than prevailing societies permit."[11] Social co-ops are not grounded in this need for utopian vision; they are grounded in the real and immediate needs of the region. What Rayman fails to mention is that the world is full of utopian visions. In a sense all human beings have a dream or fantasy of their own utopia, where everything could be just the way they want it to be. Social co-ops do not represent this desire. They are a co-operative response to the specific needs of employment, industrial development, and social change.

Social co-ops do not gather their strength from a vision of the good life. Rather their strength is in their ideological commitment to regionalism and to a socialism that favours social property above all other kinds. The success of social co-ops will depend on the vitality of these ideologies in the lives of its members. And since Western Canadian regionalism is not as powerful a force as Basque nationalism is or Zionism was, the social co-ops will reflect this. Likewise, a socialism committed primarily to co-operation is not a major movement in society and the social co-ops will also reflect this. The movement will have its weaknesses as well as its strengths.

The history of co-operation shows clearly that no matter which tradition we speak of, the creation of co-operative institutions is a struggle, a sacrifice, and a series of obstacles that must be overcome. Social co-ops must offer real benefits and rewards but they cannot offer a heaven on earth. For every achievement and gain, something is lost or surrendered and a price must be paid.

In the contemporary world the work of building communities goes on. In most cases these experiments lack both influence and longevity. In a few cases they strike a cord which shows they are in touch with history. An example of a social movement that is building new community structures is the "base community" movement among Catholics in Latin America. These "churchly congregations" as the Protestant theologian Harvey Cox calls them, meet in the homes of members. They are a combination of self-help club, community organization, and political cell.[12] They are a popular response to the revolutionary situation in Latin America because they mobilize peasants and workers around their traditional faith but in a nontraditional form that creates power for them rather than the ruling hierarchy. Cox makes it clear that these base communities, which appeared because of a lack of clergy and a new radicalism among the few that there were, cannot be copied elsewhere because those conditions do not exist elsewhere.[13] They are by and for Latin Americans.

The same would be true of social co-ops that are geared to Western Canada at this particular historical moment and arise out of the successes and failures of the liberal democratic tradition in the region. They would be the child of a specific past and a specific present and they would inherit a genetic code that makes them suited to the region.

This being in tune with the history of a particular place comes from a trust in the people of that place and their ability to pioneer. William H. Friedland confirmed this approach in outlining the factors needed to make community organization work successful. He claimed that it had to focus on a geographic area, that it had to work on resolvable problems, and that it had to depend on the action of the constituents themselves.[14] This is a far cry from the communal model of charismatic leadership. Those who first seek to establish social co-ops will find no mass movement to sweep them along or show them precisely what to do. They will find no guru to lead the way. They will have only themselves to turn to.

The task of building something that has never existed before is a awesome challenge but at least each one will know that social co-ops can only come into existence with the participation of others. One is never completely alone. That is the secret strength of co-operation. It is always a "we" situation and that includes not only the immediate colleagues working on the common project but also the silent partnership of generations of co-operators who have pointed the way.

THE SEARCH FOR COMMUNITY

NOTES

AUTHOR'S PREFACE

1. Today over two million of the 4.5 million people in the Prairie region live in cities with populations of 100,000 and up. Another half-million live in towns with populations of 25,000 and up. The rural population declined from 61.9 percent of the population in 1941 to less than 50 percent in 1971. (Roger Gibbins, *Prairie Politics and Society: Regionalism in Decline* (Toronto: Butterworths 1980), pp.17 and 68.) A 1984 Report of the Economic Council of Canada titled *Western Transition* showed that the labour force employed in agriculture in Western Canada went from 44.6 percent in 1921 to 17.8 percent in 1961 to 7.2 percent in 1981. (Ottawa: Canadian Government Publishing Centre, 1984, pp.17-18.)

2. Between 1975 and 1981 Alberta's unemployment rate hovered around 4 percent. In 1984 it was 12 percent and rising. In the construction industry unemployment was a staggering 30 percent. (*Edmonton Journal*, May 19, 1984 p.C1) High unemployment has resulted in the growth of food banks, which are the eighties counterpart of the thirties "soup kitchen." Regina and Saskatoon, whose boom was more controlled than Alberta's did not develop the 14 and 12 percent apartment vacancy rates that Calgary and Edmonton came to have. (*Edmonton Journal*, May 19, 1984 p.E1) In February 1985 Edmonton's unemployment rate hit 15.5 percent.

3. Martin Buber, "In the Midst of Crisis" in *The Writings of Martin Buber* ed. Will Herberg (New York: New American Library, 1956), p.127.

4. For a general overview there is J.F. Conway's recent book *The West: The History of a Region in Confederation* (Toronto: Lorimer, 1983). For a more detailed and biographical insight into Prairie radicalism one can read Anthony Mardiros, *William Irvine: The Life of a Prairie Radical* (Toronto: Lorimer, 1979) and Kenneth McNaught, *A Prophet in Politics: A Biography of J.S. Woodsworth* (Toronto: University of Toronto Press, 1959).

5. A good comparison of the failures of the labour movement and the successes of the farm movement can be seen in A. Ross McCormack, *Reformers, Rebels, and Revolutionnaries: The Western Canadian Radical Movement 1899-1919* (Toronto: University of Toronto Press, 1977) and Gary Fairburn, *From Prairie Roots: The Remarkable Story of the Saskatchewan Wheat Pool* (Saskatoon: Western Producer Prairie Books, 1983).

6. *Patterns and Trends of Canadian Co-operative Development* (Saskatoon: Co-operative College of Canada, 1982) p.146.

CHAPTER ONE

1. A.E. Bestor, *Journal of the History of Ideas*, IX, 3, p.259ff.

2. Ian MacPherson, *Each for All: A History of the Co-operative Movement in English Canada 1900-1945* (Toronto: Macmillan, 1979) p.6.

3. *Report of the International Co-operative Alliance Commission on Co-operative Principles* (London: ICA, 1967).

4. G. Davidovic, *Towards a Co-operative World* (Antigonish, N.S: Coady International Institute, 1967), p.12.

5. Jack Trevena, *Prairie Co-operation: A Diary* (Saskatoon: Co-operative College of Canada, 1976) p.1.

6. Davidovic, *Towards a Co-operative World*, p.30.

7. E.B. Raphael, "Social Problems of a Collective Society:The Kibbutz" in *Sociétés Villageoises: Autodeveloppement et Interco-opération* Henri Desroche et al.(Paris: Mouton, 1974) p.174.

8. Lazlo Valko, *Essays on Modern Co-operation* (Seattle: Washington State University Press, 1964), pp.3 and 6.

9. Marvin A. Schaars, *Co-operatives: Principles and Practice* (Madison: University of Wisconsin Extension, 1980), p.66.

10. Henri Desroche, *Le Developpement Intercoopératif: Ses Modèles et Ses Combinaisons* Les Cahiers de la Coopération (Sherbrooke, Que: Librairie de la Cité Université de Sherbrooke, 1969), p.100.

11. Charles Gide, *Communities and Co-operative Colonies* (London: George G. Harrap, 1930), p.199.

12. T.D. Harris, *Co-operative Principles: Their Practice, Problems and Potential in Canada*, Research Report (Winnipeg: University of Manitoba Faculty of Agriculture and Home Economics, 1968), p.222.

13. George Jacob Holyoake, *The History of Co-operation* (London: T.Fisher Unwin, 1907), pp.28-32.

14. Beatrice Potter (Mrs Sidney Webb), *The Co-operative Movement in Great Britain* (London: George Allen and Unwin, 1891), p.1.

15. "La tradition rochalienne hérité de l'associationisme pré-Rochalien enraciné lui-même dans la lignée des socialistes expérimentaux a typologie religieuse ou laïque." Henri Desroche, *Coopération et Développement: Mouvements Coopératifs et Strategie du Développement (Paris:*

Presses Universitaires de France, 1964),p.35.

16. G.D.H. Cole, *A Century of Co-operation* (Manchester: Co-operative Union, 1944), p.59.

17. Desroche in *Cooperation et Developpement* describes these stages as utopian, ideological, and demythologizing. p.121.

18. Alexander F. Laidlaw, *Co-operation in the Year 2000* (Ottawa: Co-operative Union of Canada, 1981), p.41.

19. The Co-operative Future Directions Project at York University, Toronto, in the early 1980s is a good examination of this re-examination in Canada.

20. Desroche, *Coopération et Développement*, p.123.

21. Louis Smith, *The Evolution of Agricultural Co-operation* (Oxford: Blackwell, 1961), p.112. The author calculates that in the 100 years since the first act was passed 4,000 co-operative laws have been enacted worldwide.

22. Cole, *A Century of Co-operation*, p.90.

23. Potter, *The Co-operative Movement in Great Britain*, p.70.

24. Ibid, p.119.

25. Holyoake, *History of Co-operation*, pp.357 and 620.

26. Cole, *Century of Co-operation*, p.9.

27. Laidlaw, *Co-operatives in the Year 2000*, p.9.

28. Desroche, *Coopération et Développement*. p.13. In 1960, 80 percent of the co-ops in the ICA were either consumer or credit co-ops and over half of all the members were European.

29. Laidlaw, *Co-operation in the Year 2000*, p.9.

30. Ibid., p.41.

31. Ibid., p.43.

32. Malcolm Sargent, *Agricultural Co-operation* (Aldeshot, England: Gower Publishers, 1982), p.viii.

33. Ibid., p.128.

34. Cole, *Century of Co-operation*, p.319.

35. Valko, *Essays on Modern Co-operation*, p.19.

36. Smith, *Evolution of Agricultural Co-operation*, p.161.

37. J. Erasmus, *In Search of the Common Good: Utopian Experiments Past and Future* (New York: The Free Press, 1977), pp.115-118.

38. Benjamin Zablocki, *Alienation and Charisma: A Study of Contemporary American Communes* (New York: The Free Press, 1980), p.3.

39. Laurence Veysey, *The Communal Experience: Anarchist and Mystical Communities in Twentieth Century America* (Chicago: University of Chicago Press, 1978), p.vii.

40. *Private interview with Prof. Desroche in Paris, September 29, 1983.*

CHAPTER TWO

1. G.D.H. Cole, *The British Co-operative Movement in a Socialist Society* (London: George Allen and Unwin, 1951), p.34.

2. Quoted in Malcolm Sargent, *Agricultural Co-operation* (Aldeshot, England: Gower Publishers, 1982), p.73.

3. Ibid., p.149.

4. G.D.H. Cole, *A Century of Co-operation* (Manchester: Co-operative Union, 1944), p.12.

5. Alexander Laidlaw, *Co-operatives in the Year 2000* (Ottawa: Co-operative Union of Canada, 1981), p.41.

6. Henrik F. Infield, *Utopia and Experiment: Essays in the Sociology of Co-operation* (New York: Praeger, 1955), p.159.

7. Louis Smith, *The Evolution of Agricultural Co-operation* (Oxford: Blackwell, 1961), p.148.

8. Sargent, *Agricultural Co-operation*, p.1.

9. Cole, *Century of Co-operation*, p.356.

10. Ibid., p.255.

11. Smith, *Evolution of Agricultural Co-operation*, mentions some of these splits on p.149 and Cole, *Century of Co-operation*, describes the divisions pp.352-365. Desroche, *Coopération et Développement*, lists the debates from 1895 to 1960 pp.154-165.

12. Valko, *Essays in Modern Co-operation*, p.14.

13. Laidlaw, *Co-operatives in the Year 2000*, p.42.

14. Valko, *Essays in Modern Co-operation*, p.47.

15. *A Co-operative Development Strategy for Canada*, Report of the National Task Force on Co-operative Development, May 1984. (Ottawa: Co-operative Housing Foundation, 1984) p.10.

16. Henri Desroche, *Le Développement Intercoopératif: Ses Modèles et Ses Combinaison*, Les Cahiers de la Coopération (Sherbrooke, Que: Librairie de la cité Université de Sherbrooke, 1969) listed Canada as having 28 percent of its population holding membership in co-ops during the 1960s. Today that figure is over 40 percent, which would put Canada in the top third of countries with co-ops.

17. *Financial Post*, March 24, 1984, p.40 and *CUC News Service*, Vol.6, No.3, Feb. 15, 1985. p.3.

18. *Patterns and Trends of Canadian Co-operative Development* (Saskatoon: Co-operative College of Canada, 1982), p.12.

19. *Co-operative Outlooks* (Saskatoon: Co-operative College of Canada, 1983), p.31.

20. John E. Jordan et al., *The Co-operative Sector*, CFDP Working Papers (Saskatoon: Co-operative College of Canada, 1982), p.29.

21. M. Laflamme et al., *Le Projet Co-operatif Quebecois: Un Projet Social?* (Chicoutimi, Que: Gaetan Morin, 1982), p.100.

NOTES

22. *Patterns and Trends*, p.24.

23. *Financial Post*, March 24, 1984, p.40.

24. *Globe and Mail*, May 30, 1984, p.B9.

25. *Co-operative Outlooks*, p.54.

26. Terry Phalen, *Co-operative Leadership: Harry Fowler* (Saskatoon: Co-operative College of Canada, 1977), p.v.

27. J.F. Conway, *The West: The History of a Region in Confederation* (Toronto: Lorimer, 1983), pp.45-6.

28. V.C. Fowke, *The National Policy and the Wheat Economy* (Toronto: University of Toronto Press, 1957), p.103.

29. A.B. McKillop, ed., *Contexts of Canada's Past: Selected Essays of W.L. Morton* (Toronto: Macmillan, 1980), p.151.

30. Roger Gibbins, *Prairie Politics and Society: Regionalism in Decline* (Toronto: Butterworths, 1981) p.17.

31. Ian MacPherson, *The Co-operative Movement on the Prairies 1900-1955*, Booklet No. 33 (Ottawa: Canadian Historical Assoc., 1979), p.6.

32. *Financial Post*, March 24, 1984, p.20.

33. Jordan,*Co-operative Sector*, p.28.

34. *Tenth Annual Report, Saskatchewan Co-operative Wheat Producers Limited*, Regina, 1934, p.62.

35. *Patterns and Trends*, p.39.

36. Gibbins, *Prairie Politics and Society*, p.78.

37. Ibid., p.79.

38. *Globe and Mail*, April 9, 1984, p.B2.

39. Ibid.

40. *Patterns and Trends*, p.70.

41. Ibid., p.146.

42. T.D. Harris, *Co-operative Principles: Their Practice, Problems, and Potential in Canada*, A Research Report (Winnipeg: University of Manitoba Faculty of Agriculture and Home Economics, 1968), p.129.

43. A. F. Laidlaw, "Co-operatives in the Canadian Environment," in *Economic Efficiency and Democratic Control* Proceedings of a Conference (Saskatoon: Co-operative College of Canada, 1977), p.11.

44. *Patterns and Trends*, p.54.

45. Interview with Mr. Grant Mitchell, April 24, 1984 in Regina, Saskatchewan.

46. Ian MacPherson, *Each for All: A History of the Co-operative Movement in English Canada 1900-1945* (Toronto: Macmillan, 1979), p.106.

47. Gibbins, *Prairie Politics and Society*, pp.81 and 87.

48. See W.L. Morton's essay "The Social Philosophy of Henry Wise Wood" in McKillop, *Contexts of Canada's Past*, pp.113-138, and Kenneth McNaught, *A Prophet in Politics: A Biography of J.S. Woodsworth* (Toronto:

University of Toronto Press, 1959) provide useful insights into each man.

49. See John Richards and Larry Pratt, *Prairie Capitalism* (Toronto: McClelland and Stewart, 1979) for a full treatment of the changes to the prairie economy in the postwar period.

50. Some writings on ideology are: John Plamenatz, *Ideology* (London: Macmillan, 1970); M. Seliger, *Ideology and Politics* (New York: Free Press, 1976); L.B. Brown, *Ideology* (London: Penguin, 1975). These books review most of the viewpoints on what constitutes ideology.

51. George Rude, *Ideology and Popular Protest* (New York: Pantheon, 1980), p.161.

52. John Jordan, *Co-operative Movements, Systems, and Futures*, CFDP Working Papers No.2 (Saskatoon: Co-operative College of Canada, 1981), p.4.

53. *Patterns and Trends*, p.101.

CHAPTER THREE

1. ''Manifesto of the Communist Party'' in Karl Marx and Frederick Engels, *Selected Works* (Moscow: Progress Publishers, 1970), p.60.

2. Ralph Miliband, *Marxism and Politics* (Oxford: Oxford University Press, 1977) quotes Marx's colleague Frederick Engels' October 23, 1846 letter as defining the objects of the Communists as: ''1) to achieve the interests of the proletariat in opposition to those of the bourgeoisie ; 2) to do this through the abolition of private property and its replacement by community of goods; 3) to recognize no means of carrying out these objects other than a democratic revolution by force.'' p.21.

3. For a simplified explanation of Marx's theory of dialectical or historical materialism see Maurice Cornforth, *Materialism and the Dialectical Method*, 4th ed.(New York: International Publishers, 1971).

4. Miliband, *Marxism and Politics*, p.113.

5. Charles J. Erasmus, *In Search of the Common Good: Utopian Experiments Past and Future* (New York: The Free Press, 1977) gives a figure of 80 percent. p.240.

6. Ibid., p.241.

7. Karl Eugen Wadekin, ''The Soviet Kolkhoz: Vehicle of Co-operative Farming or of Control and Transfer of Resources?'' in Peter Dorner ed., *Co-operative and Commune: Group Farming in the Economic Development of Agriculture* (Madison, Wis: University of Wisconsin Press, 1977), p.96.

8. Paul R. Gregory and Robert C. Stuart, *Soviet Economic Structure and Performance* (New York: Harper and Row, 1982) p.225.

9. Erasmus, *In Search of the Common Good*, p.254.

10. Gregory and Stuart, *Soviet Economic Structure and Performance*, p.103.

11. Statistics for the famine are difficult to come by since the Russian government first denied it existed and then attributed it to natural

causes. The official figure provided to Stalin was 3.5 million. (Quoted in M.Scammel, *Solzhenitsyn*(New York: W.W. Norton, 1984) p.74. In 1946 the League of Nations gave a figure of 6 to 7 million and Samir Amin says 13 million in *The Future of Maoism* (New York, Monthly Review Press, 1982).

12. Robert C. Stuart, *The Collective Farm in Soviet Agriculture* (Lexington, Mass: D.C. Heath and Co., 19) p.199.

13. Wadekin, "The Soviet Kolkhoz" p.101.

14. Samir Amin, *The Future of Maoism*, trans. N. Finkelstein (New York: Monthly Review Press, 1982), p.79.

15. Erasmus, *In Search of the Common Good*, p.234.

16. Ibid., p.255.

17. Wadekin, "The Soviet Kolkhoz", p.102.

18. Gregory and Stuart, *Soviet Economic Structure and Performance*, p.234.

19. Ibid., p.225.

20. Ibid.

21. Ibid., p.239.

22. Ibid., p.241.

23. Ibid., p.240.

24. Henrik F. Infield, *Utopia and Experiment: Essays in the Sociology of Co-operation* (New York: Praeger, 1955), p.128.

25. Ibid., pp.130 and 140.

26. Nym Wales, *China Builds for Democracy: A Story of Co-operative Industry* (New York: Modern Ages Books, 1941), pp.V&VI.

27. Ibid., p.41.

28. Ibid., p.83.

29. Ibid., p.247.

30. Central Committee of the Communist Party of China, ed., *Socialist Upsurge in China's Countryside* (Beijing: Foreign Languages Press, 1978), p.2.

31. Audrey Donnithorne, *China's Economic System* (London: Allen and Unwin, 1967), p.41.

32. Rene Dumont, *Chine Surpeuplee: Tiers-Monde Afflame* (Paris: Editions du Seuil, 1965), p.41

33. Bill Brugger, *China: Liberation and Transformation 1942-1962* (London: Croom Helm, 1981), p.125; S. Amin, *Future of Maoism*, p.58; Erasmus, *In Search of the Common Good*, p.240; and John Wong, "Communalization of Peasant Agriculture: China's Organizational Strategy for Agricultural Development" in Peter Dorner, ed., *Co-operative and Commune*, p.117.

34. *Socialist Upsurge*, p.511.

35. Ibid., p.26.

36. Rene Dumont, *Chine: La Revolution Culturelle* (Paris: Editions du Seuil, 1976), pp.23 and 26. Donnithorne, *China's Economic System*, gives a figureof 26,400 communes, p.46.

37. Dumont, *Chine Surpeuplee*, p.73.

38. Donnithorne, *China's Economic System*, p.511.

39. For a first-hand acount of Ya'nan see Edgar Snow, *Red Star over China*.

40. Brugger, *China: Liberation and Transformation*, p.191.

41. Dumont, *Chine: La Revolution Culturelle*, p.56.

42. Wong, "Communalization of Peasant Agriculture", p.117.

43. Dumont, *Chine Surpeuplee*, p.61.

44. Brugger, *China: Liberation and Transformation*, p.254.

45. Samir Amin, *The Future of Maoism*, p.48. H provides the following comparative figures for per capita percentage growth: China 5.2; India 1.1.; Pakistan 1.4; Bangladesh -0.5; U.S.S.R. 3.8; U.S. 2.9 for the period 1960 to 1974. These are World Bank figures., p.75.

46. Ibid., p.57.

47. Ibid., p.69.

48. Milovan Djilas, *Tito: The Story From Inside*, trans. V. Kojic and R. Hayes (New York: Harcourt, Brace, Jovanovich, 1980), p.35.

49. Ibid., p.74.

50. Branko Horvat, "The Labor-Managed Enterprise" in Branko Horvat et al., ed., *Self-Governing Socialism*, Vol. Two (White Plains, New York: International Arts and Science Press Inc., 1970), p.129.

51. I. Maksimovic "The Economic System and Workers' Self-Management in Yugoslavia" in M.J. Brockmeyer, ed., *Yugoslav Workers' Self-Management* (Dordrecht, Holland: Reidel, 1970), p.129.

52. H.D. Seibel and U.G. Damachi, *Self-Management in Yugoslavia and the Developing World* (London: Macmillan Press, 1982), p.3.

53. R. Supek "The Sociology of Workers' Self-Management" in *Self- Governing Socialism*, p.4.

54. Horvat "The Labor-Managed Enterprise" in *Self-Governing Socailism* , p.165.

55. Josip Obradovic and William N. Dunn, ed., *Workers' Self- Management and Organizational Power in Yugoslavia* (Pittsburgh: University of Pittsburgh, 1978), p.5.

56. Ibid., p.16. J. Zupanove "Participation and Influences" in *Self-Governing Socialism* quotes one 1960s survey as showing a low level of worker participation. p.82.

57. Stephen R. Sacks "Giant Corporations in Yugoslavia" in D.C.Jones and J. Svejma, ed., *Participatory and Self-Managed Firms: Evaluating Economic Performance* (Toronto: D.C. Heath, 1982), pp.113 and 117.

58. S. Estrin and William Bartlett "The Effects of Enterprise Self-

Management in Yugoslavia: An Empirical Survey" in *Participatory and Self-Managed Firms*, p.94.

59. J. Zupanov in *Workers Self-Management and Organizational Power*, p.71.

60. Ibid.

61. M. Cornford writes in *Materialism and the Dialectical Method* "The producer.enjoys.a share of the social product 'according to his work' in the first stage of communist society and 'according to his needs' in the fully developed communist society." p.119.

62. George G. Wang, ed. *Fundamentals of Poltical Economcy* (White Plains, N.Y: M.E. Sharpe Inc., 1977), p.297.

63. Ibid., p.283.

CHAPTER FOUR

1. Alan Taylor, *Democratic Planning Through Workers' Control*, (London: Socialist Environmental and Resource Association, n.d.), p.8.

2. Menachem Gerson, *Family, Women, and Socialization in the Kibbutz* (Toronto, D.C. Heath, 1978), p.2.

3. Paula Rayman, *The Kibbutz Community and Nation Building* (Princeton, N.J: Princeton University Press, 1981), p.4.

4. Julius K. Nyerere, *Freedom and Socialism: A Selection from Writings and Speeches 1965-1967* (Dar Es Salaam: Oxford University Press, 1968), p.2.

5. Robert Oakeshott, *The Case for Workers Co-ops* (London: Routledge and Kegan Paul, 1978), p.xv.

6. Ibid., p.251.

7. Peter Jay "The Workers Co-operative Economy" in Alasdair Clayre, ed., *Political Economy of Co-operation and Participation* (London: Oxford University Press, 1980), p.9.

8. H. Darin-Drabin, *The Other Society* (London: Victor Gollancz, 1962), p.60.

9. Ibid., p.77.

10. J. Erasmus, *In Search of the Common Good: Utopian Experiments Past and Future* (New York: The Free Press, 1977), p.175. In 1936 there were 47 kibbutzim with a population of 10,575; in 1951 there were 189 kibbutzim with a population of 64,523; and in 1972 there were 235 with a population of 101,103. These statistics are cited in Avner Ben-Ner "Changing Values and Preferences in Communal Organization: Econometric Evidence from the Experience of the Israeli Kibbutz" in Derek C. Jones and Jan Svejmar, eds., *Participatory and Self-Managed Firms* (Toronto: D. C. Heath) pp.260-61.

11. *Globe and Mail*, February 19, 1983. That 3.5 percent of the population also supplies 25 percent of Israel's army officers.

12. Harry Viteles, *History of the Co-operative Movement in Israel* Vol.1 (London: Vallentine and Mitchell, 1967), pp.259-60.

13. Darin-Drabkin, *The Other Society*, p.307.
14. Rayman, *The Kibbutz Community*, pp.28 and 75.
15. Darin-Drabkin, *The Other Society*, p.291.
16. Keith Sapsin Fine, "Worker Participation in Israel" in G. Hunnius et al., eds., *Workers Control: A Reader in Labor and Social Change* (New York: Vintage Books, 1973), p.245.
17. Rayman, *The Kibbutz Community*, p.85.
18. Darin-Drabkin, *The Other Society*, pp.276 and 282 and Rayman, *The Kibbutz Community*, p.99.
19. Menachem Rosner, "Self-Management in Kibbutz Industry: Organizational Patterns and Determinants of Psychological Effects" in U. Leviathan and M. Rosner, eds., *Work and Organization in Kibbutz Industry* (Darby, Pa: Norwood Editions, 1982), p.159.
20. Menachem Rosner, "Overview", Ibid., p.xiv.
21. Amia Lieblich, *Kibbutz Makom: Report from an Israeli Kibbutz* (London: Andre Deutsch, 1982), p.xx.
22. Ibid., p.192.
23. Melford E. Spiro, *Kibbutz: Venture in Utopia* (New York: Schocken Books, 1970), p.25.
24. Darin-Drabkin, *The Other Society*, p.83.
25. Golda Meir, *My Life* (New York: G.P. Putnam, 1975), p.48.
26. Harry Viteles, *History of the Co-operative Movement in Israel* Vol.2, p.11.
27. Yehuda Don, "Dynamics of Development in the Israeli Kibbutz" in P. Dorner, ed., *Co-operative and Commune* (Madison, Wis: University of Wisconsin Press, 1977), p.49.
28. Erasmus, *In Search of the Common Good*, p.168, and Lieblich, *Kibbutz Makom*, p.249.
29. J. Quarter, "Intergenerational Discontinuity in the Israeli Kibbutz," unpublished paper, 1984.
30. Rayman, *The Kibbutz Community*, p.253.
31. Yehuda Don, "Dynamics of Development" in *Co-operative and Commune*, p.61.
32. Leviathan and Rosner, *Work and Organization in Kibbutz Industry* , p.191.
33. Erasmus, *In Search of the Common Good*, p.196.
34. Gerson in *Women and Socialization in the Kibbutz* states that of 88 kibbutzim in the Ichud federation, 67 had children sleeping with parents by the mid-70s. p.53.
35. Don, "Dynamics of Development" in *Co-operative and Commune*, p.61.
36. Ibid.
37. Nyerere, *Freedom and Socialism*, p.3.
38. Ibid., p.232.
39. D.E. McHenry Jr., *Tanzania's Ujamaa Villages: The Implementation of a*

NOTES

Rural Development Strategy (Berkeley, Calif: University of California Press, 1979), p.2.

40. B.U. Mwansasu and Cranford Pratt, "Tanzania's Strategy for the Transition to Socialism" in Mwansasu and Pratt, eds., *Towards Socialism in Tanzania* (Toronto: University of Toronto Press, 1979), p.7.

41. J. Boesen, B.S. Madsen, and T. Moody, *Ujamaa—Socialism from Above* (Uppsala: Scandinavian Institute of African Studies, 1977), p.15.

42. M. von Freyhold, *Ujamaa Villages in Tanzania: Analysis of a Social Experiment* (London: Heineman, 1979), p.22.

43. McHenry, *Tanzania's Ujamaa Villages, pp.133 and 212.*

44. *M. von Freyhold, Ujamaa Villages in Tanzania*, pp.111 and 115.

45. Boesen, von Freyhold, and Shivji are the Marxist critics.

46. Issa G. Shivji, *Class Struggle in Tanzania* (New York: Monthly Review Press, 1976), pp. 18 and 83.

47. M. von Freyhold, *Ujamaa Villages in Tanzania*, pp.60-61.

48. See Sam Dolgoff, ed., *The Anarchist Collectives: Workers Self- Management in the Spanish Revolution 1936-1939* (Montreal: Black Rose Books, 1974) and Gaston Leval, *Collectives in the Spanish Revolution* (London: Freedom Press, 1975).

49. Augustin Souchy, "Economic Structure and Coordination" in Dolgoff, *The Anarchist Collectives*, p.66.

50. Daniel Guerin, *L'anarchisme* (Paris: Gallimard, 1965), p.157.

51. Ibid., p.164.

52. Roger Spear, "The Mondragon Co-operative Experience" in *Mondragon Co-operatives—Myth and Model* (United Kingdom: Open University, 1982), p.18.

53. Christopher S. Axworthy, "Worker Co-operatives in Mondragon, the U.K., and France: Some Reflections" Occasional Paper 85-01, Feb. 1985 (Saskatoon: Centre for the Study of Co-operatives, University of Saskatchewan), p.19.

54. Bob Milbrath, "Lessons From the Mondragon Co-ops" in *Science for the People*, Vol.15, No.3, May/June 1983, p.11.

55. John Jordan, "The Mondragon Experiment" in *Perception*, Feb. 1982, p.29. Henk Thomas and Chris Logan, *Mondragon: An Economic Analysis* (London: George Allen and Unwin, 1982), p.91.

56. Milbrath, "Lessons from the Mondragon Co-ops", p.29.

57. Thomas and Logan, *Mondragon*, p.175.

58. Ibid., p.76 and Jordan, "The Mondragon Experiment", p.28.

59. Robert Oakeshott, "Capital Stakes at Corby" in Spear, *Mondragon Co-operatives*, p.65.

60. Oakeshott, *The Case for Workers Co-ops*, p.243. Hendrik Thomas, "The Performance of the Mondragon Co-operatives in Spain" in Jones and Svejmar, *Participatory and Self-Managed Firms"*, p.129 and 151.

61. Robert P. Clark, *The Basques: The Franco Years and Beyond* (Reno: University of Nevada Press, 1979), p.9.

62. Robert O'Connor and Philip Kelly, *A Study of Industrial Workers Co-operatives* (Dublin: The Economic and Social Research Institute, 1980), p.6.

63. Jenny Thornley, *Worker Co-operatives: Jobs and Dreams* (London: Heineman, 1981), p.2.

64. Linda Wintner, "Employee Buyouts: An Alternative to Plant Closing", Research Bulletin #140 (New York: Conference Board Inc., 1983), p.14.

65. *Business Week*, March 28, 1983, p.39.

66. Wintner, "Employee Buyouts", pp.3 and 4.

67. Tove Hammer et al., *Worker Participation and Ownership: Co-operative Strategies for Strengthening Local Economies* (Ithica, N.Y: I.L.R. Press, 1982), p.9.

68. *Business Week*, "Revolution or Rip-off?", April 15, 1985, pp.94-108.

69. Paul Bernstein, *Workplace Democratization: Its Internal Dynamics* (New Brunswick, N.J: Transaction Books, 1976), p.13.

70. Keith Bradley and Alan Gelb, *Worker Capitalism: The New Industrial Relations* (Cambridge, Mass: MIT Press, 1984), p.69.

71. Ibid.

72. Jack Quarter, "Worker Coops in English Canada 1984: A Movement in the Making" in J.E. Jordan and J. Quarter, "Worker Cooperatives" Working Papers Vol.2, No.6 (Saskatoon: Co-operative College of Canada ,1984).

73. See Canada's *Worker Co-op Newsletter*, Vol.4, #1 and 2.

74. *A Co-operative Development Strategy for Canada* Report of the National Task Force on Co-operative Development, May 1984 (Ottawa: Co-operative Housing Foundation, 1984), p.xvi.

CHAPTER FIVE

1. John A. Hostetler, *Communitarian Societies* (New York: Holt, Rinehard, and Winston, 1974), p.2.

2. Ibid., p.19.

3. Laurence Veysey, *The Communal Experience: Anarchist and Mystical Communities in Twentieth Century America* (Chicago: University of Chicago Press, 1978), p.vii and 52. Rosabeth Moss Kanter, *Commitment and Community: Communes and Utopias in Sociological Perspective* (Cambridge, Mass: Harvard University Press, 1972), p.32.

4. J.F.C. Harrison, *Robert Owen and the Owenites in Britain and America: The Quest for the New Moral World* (London: Routledge and Kegan Paul, 1969), p.136.

5. Charles J. Erasmus, *In Search of the Common Good: Utopian Experiments Past and Future* (New York: The Free Press, 1977), p.47.

6. P. Abrams et al., *Communes, Sociology, and Society* (London: Cambridge University Press, 1976), p.36.

7. Kanter, *Commitment and Community*, p.65.

8. J.A. Hostetler and G.E. Huntington, *The Hutterites in North America* (New York: Holt, Rinehart, and Winston, 1967), pp. 11-12.

9. H.B. Workman, *The Evolution of the Monastic Ideal* (Boston: Beacon Press, 1962), p.154.

10. Erasmus, *In Search of the Common Good*, p.123.

11. Francis J. Moloney, *Free to Love: Poverty, Chastity, and Obedience* (London: Darton, Longman, and Todd, 1981), p.18.

12. Interview with Andrew Britz O.S.B. of St. Peter's Abbey, Muenster, Sask., April 17, 1984.

13. Alejandro Cussianovich, *Religious Life and the Poor: Liberation Theology*, trans. John Drury (New York: Orbis Books, 1979), p.24.

14. Demetrius Dumm O.S.B., "Monasticism and Contemporary Culture" in *American Benedictine Review*, Vol.26, No.2, June 1975, p.130.

15. Richard Endress, "The Monastery as a Liminal Community" in *American Benedictine Review* Vol.26, No.2, June, 1975, p.144.

16. Ibid., pp.154 and 174.

17. Kanter, *Commitment and Community*, p.3.

18. Erasmus, *In Search of the Common Good*, p.124.

19. Kenneth Rexroth, *Communalism: From its Origins to the Twentieth Century*, (New York: Seabury Press, 1974), p.205.

20. Ibid., p.212.

21. Quoted in Kanter, *Commitment and Community*, p.9.

22. Rexroth, *Communalism*, p.180.

23. Donald E. Pitzer and Josephine M. Elliot, "New Harmony's First Utopians" in *Indiana Magazine of History*, Vol.LXXV, No.3, September 1979, p.230.

24. Rexroth, *Communalism*, p.217.

25. Harrison, *Robert Owen and the Owenites*, p.154.

26. Rexroth, *Communalism*, p.219.

27. Harrison, *Robert Owen and the Owenites*, p.47.

28. William Hedgepath and Dennise Stock, *The Alternative: Communal Life in New America* (New York: Macmillan, 1970), p.5.

29. Veysey, *The Communal Experience*, p.7.

30. David Moberg, "Experimenting with the Future: Alternative Institutions and American Socialism" in John Case and Rosemary Taylor, *Co-ops, Communes and Collectives: Experiments in Social Change in the 1960s and 1970s* (New York: Pantheon Books, 1979), p.285.

31. Kanter, *Commitment and Community*, p.72 and p.129.

32. Bennet M. Berger, *The Survival of a Counterculture* (Berkeley: University

of California Press, 1981), pp.18 and 29.

33. Gilbert Zicklin, *Countercultural Commune: A Sociological Perspective*, (Westport, Conn: Greenwood Press, 1983), p.xiii.

34. Bejamin Zablocki, *A Study of Contemporary American Communes* (New York: The Free Press, 1980), p.4.

35. David Moberg, "Experimenting with the Future" in *Co-ops, Communes and Collectives*, p.285.

36. Paul Starr, "The Phantom Community" in *Co-ops, Communes, and Collectives*, p.267.

37. Novia Carter, *Something of Promise: The Canadian Communes* (Ottawa: Canadian Council on Social Development, 1974), p.38.

38. For a recent assessment of the monastery and its impact see Bede Hubbard, "St. Peter's: A German-American Marriage of Monastery and Colony" in B.G. Smillie, ed., *Visions of the New Jerusalem: Religious Settlement on the Prairies* (Edmonton: NeWest Press, 1983), pp.153-164.

39. I am indebted to the Rev. Andrew Britz O.S.B. of St. Peter's Abbey for this description of the workings of the abbey.

40. Koozma J. Tarasoff, "The Western Settlement of the Canadian Doukhobours" in *Visions of the New Jerusalem*, p.124.

41. George Woodcock and Ivan Avakumovic, *The Doubkhobours* (London: Faber and Faber, 1968), p.12.

42. Ibid., p.136.

43. John Ryan, *The Agricultural Economy of Manitoba Hutterite Colonies* (Toronto: McClelland and Stewart, 1976), p.274.

44. Hostetler and Huntington, *Hutterites in North America*, p.110.

45. J.A. Hostetler, *Hutterite Society* (Baltimore: Johns Hopkins University Press, 1974), p.273.

46. John W. Bennet, "The Hutterian Colony: A Traditional Voluntary Commune with Large Economic Scale" in P. Dorner, ed.,*Co-ops and Communes* (Madison, Wis: University of Wisconsin Press, 1977), p.73.

47. Ryan, *The Agricultural Economy of Manitoba Hutterite Colonies*, p.230.

48. Ibid., p.275.

49. Robert J. MacDonald, "Hutterite Education in Alberta: A Test Case in Assimilation" in A.W. Rasporich, ed. *Western Canada: Past and Present* (Toronto: McClelland and Stewart, 1975), p.148.

50. I am indebted for my information on this settlement to Gilbert Johnson, "The Harmony Industrial Association: A Pioneer Co-operative" in *Saskatchewan History*, Vol.4, No.1, 1954, pp.11-20.

51. Interview with Mr. Lorne Dietrick, Matador, Sask., April 26, 1984.

52. Henrik F. Infield, *Utopia and Experiment: Essays in the Sociology of Co-operation* (New York: Praeger, 1955), p.114.

53. Interview with Mr. Victor Hay, Saskatoon, Sask., April 16, 1984.

54. Rexroth, *Communalism*, p.282.

55. Ibid., p.297.

56. Infield, *Utopia and Experiment*, p.17.

57. Gail McConnell, "Hutterites: An Interview with Michael Entz" in Smillie, *Visions of the New Jerusalem*, p.168.

CHAPTER SIX

1. Jenny Thornley, *Worker's Cooperatives: Jobs and Dreams* (London: Heineman, 1981), p.1.

2. Robert O'Connor and Philip Kelly, *A Study of Industrial Workers' Co-operatives* (Dublin: Economic and Social Research Institute, 1980), p.93.

3. Karl-Eugen Wadekin, "The Soviet Kolkhoz: Vehicle of Co-operative Farming or Control and Transfer of Resources?" in Peter Dorner, ed., *Co-operative and Commune* (Madison: University of Wisconsin Press, 1977), p.95. Robert C. Stuart, *The Collective Farm in Soviet Agriculture* (Toronto: D.C. Heath), p.78.

4. Lazlo Valko, *Essays on Modern Co-operation* (Seattle: Washington State University Press, 1964), p.14.

5. *Report of the International Co-operative Alliance Commission on Co-operative Principles* (Geneva: ICA), pp. 1 and 10.

6. A.F. Laidlaw, *Co-operatives in the Year 2000* (Ottawa: Co-op Union of Canada, 1981), pp.36 and 45.

7. J. G. Craig, *Philosophy, Principles and Ideology of Co-operation: What are Their Implications for a Vision of the Future* (Saskatoon: Co-operative College of Canada, 1980), p.1.

8. H. Desroche, *Co-operation et Developpement* (Paris: Presse Universitaire de France, 1964), p.153.

9. Louis Smith, *The Evolution of Agricultural Co-operatives* (Oxford: Blackwell, 1961), p.132.

10. Valko, *Essays on Modern Co-operation*, p.15.

11. Bill Brugger, *China: Liberation and Transformation 1942-1962* (London: Croom Helm, 1981), p.123.

12. Thornley, *Worker Co-operatives*, p.2.

13. Robert Oakeshott, *The Case for Workers Co-ops* (London: Routledge and Kegan Paul, 1978), p.35.

14. A.F. Laidlaw, *The Co-operative Alternative*, Co-op Future Directions Working Paper No.9 (Saskatoon: Cooperative College of Canada, 1981), p.22.

15. John Jordan, *Co-operative Movement, Systems, and Future* CFDPWP No.2 (Saskatoon: Co-operative College of Canada, 1981), p.13.

16. *Patterns and Trends of Canadian Co-operative Development* (Saskatoon: Co-operative College of Canada, 1982) p.145.

17. *A Co-operative Development Strategy for Canada* (Ottawa: Co-operative Housing Foundation, 1984) p.xvi.

18. Interview with Mr. O.E. Turnbull, Saskatoon, Sask., April 17, 1984.

19. A.F. Laidlaw, "Co-operatives in the Canadian Environment" in *Economic Efficiency and Democratic Control* (Saskatoon: Co-operative College of Canada, 1977), p.13.

20. *Patterns and Trends*, p.71.

21. T.D. Harris, *Co-operative Principles: Their Practice, Problems and Potential in Canada* (Winnipeg: University of Manitoba, 1968), p.13.

22. *Patterns and Trends*, p.101.

23. Interview with Mr. Skip Kutz, Co-op College of Canada, Saskatoon, Sask., April 6, 1984.

24. M. Laflamme, *Le Projet Co-opératif Québecois: Un projet social?* (Chicoutimi, Qué: Gaétan Morin, 1982), p.150.

25. H. Darin-Drabkin, *The Other Society* (London: Victor Gollancz, 1962), p.11.

26. *Edmonton Journal*, August 29, 1984, p.F10.

27. Economic Council of Canada, *On the Mend: Twentieth Annual Review* (Ottawa: Canadian Government Publishing Centre, 1983), p.14.

28. Quoted in Gregory Baum and Duncan Cameron, *Ethics and Economics: Canadian Catholic Bishops on the Economic Crisis* (Toronto: Lorimer, 1983), p.6.

29. *Edmonton Journal*, April 9, 1984, p.B1.

30. *Globe and Mail*, Feb.6, 1984, p.B8.

31. *Globe and Mail*, January 28, 1985, p.B6.

32. Paul Gingrich, "Decline of the Family Wage" in *Perception*, Vol.7, No.5, May/August 1984, pp.16-17.

33. Laidlaw, *Co-operatives in the Year 2000* (Ottawa: Co-operative Union of Canada, 1981), p.15.

34. *Globe and Mail*, March 5, 1984, p.B1.

35. See John Richards and Larry Pratt, *Prairie Capitalism: Power and Influence in the New West* (Toronto: McClelland and Stewart, 1979) for a study of these changes.

36. J.F. Conway, *The West: The History of a Region in Confederation* (Toronto: Lorimer, 1983), p.225.

37. Larry Pratt and Garth Stevenson, *Western Separatism* (Edmonton: Hurtig, 1981) is a treatment of the resurgence of separatist feelings.

38. For a fuller treatment of this issue see my essay "The Quiet Revolution in the West" in George Melnyk, *Radical Regionalism*, (Edmonton: NeWest Press, 1981), pp.88-96.

39. See R. Gibbins, *Prairie Politics and Society: Regionalism in Decline* (Toronto: Butterworths, 1980).

40. *On the Mend*, p.9.

41. *New York Times*, December 30, 1984, p.Y12.

CHAPTER SEVEN

1. A.F. Laidlaw, *Co-operatives in the Year 2000* (Ottawa: Co-operative Union of Canada, 1981), p.32.

2. John Jordan, *Developing Worker Co-operatives* (Saskatoon: Co-operative College of Canada,1981), p.36.

3. Donald Atlman and Douglas Holland, *Potential Contributions That Established Co-operatives Could Make to Help Solve Problems in Emerging Co-ops* CFDP (Toronto: York University, 1981).

4. Allen Abel, "Profit Motive to Propel Chinese Line" *Globe and Mail*, Feb.4, 1985, p.B13.

5. Charles Erasmus,*In Search of the Common Good: Utopian Experiments Past and Future* (New York: The Free Press, 1977), p.118.

6. Julius K Nyerere, *Freedom and Socialism: A Selection from Writings and Speeches 1965-67* (Dar Es Salaam: Oxford University Press, 1968), pp.142 and 303.

7. Harry Viteles, *A History of the Co-operative Movement in Israel* Volume Two (London: Vallentine and Mitchell, 1967), p.195.

8. Henrik Infield, *Utopia and Experiment: Essays in the Sociology of Co-operation* (New York: Praeger, 1955), p.17.

9. J. Tanner et al., "Youth Unemployment and Moral Panics" in *Perception*, Vol.7 No.5, May 1984, states that the national unemployment rate among males aged 15 to 24 was 20.6 percent in January, 1984.

10. Leah Cohen, *Small Expectations: Society's Betrayal of Older Women* (Toronto: McClelland and Stewart, 1984).

11. Jane O'Hara, "Parents Without Partners" *Macleans*, October 15, 1984, p.60.

12. Gayle Kimball, *The 50-50 Marriage* (Boston: Beacon Press, 1983), p.5.

13. Dolores Hayden, *Redesigning the American Dream: The Future of Housing, Work, and Family Life* (New York: W.W. Norton, 1984), pp. 170 and 197.

14. Menachem Gerson, *Family, Women, and Socialization in the Kibbutz* (D.C. Heath, Toronto, 1978), p.48.

15. Baker Brownell, *The Human Community: Its Philosophy and Practice for a Time of Crisis* (New York: Harper, 1950), p.33.

16. Rene Konig, *The Community* (New York: Schocken Books, 1968), pp.18-20.

17. William Herberg, ed., *The Writings of Martin Buber* (New York: New American Library, 1956),p.133.

18. Brownell, *The Human Community*, p.115.

19. M. Beha, *The Dynamics of Community* (New York: Corpus Books, 1970), p.12.

20. Joseph R. Blasi, *The Communal Future: The Kibbutz and the Utopian Dilemma* (Norwood, Pa: Norwood Editions, 1980), p.viii.

21. Ibid., p.ix.

22. Nyerere, *Freedom and Socialism*, p.351.
23. Atlman and Holland, *Potential Contributions*, p.24.

CHAPTER EIGHT

1. David H. Wright, *Co-operatives and Community: The Theory and Practice of Producer Co-operatives* (London: Bedford Square Press, 1980), pp.16-18.
2. Charles Gide, *Communist and Co-operative Colonies* (London: George G. Harrap, 1930), pp.55 and 56.
3. G. Davidovic, *Towards a Co-operative World* (Antigonish, N.S. Coady International Institute, 1967), p.48.
4. Dr. H. Darin-Drabkin, *The Other Society* (London: Victor/Gollancz, 1962), p.315.
5. Jaroslav Vanek, "Toward a Forward Step in Empirical Self-Management Research" in Derek C. Jones and Jan Svejma eds, *Participatory and Self-Managed Firms (Lexington, Mass: D.C. Heath, 1982)*
6. Henk Thomas and Chris Logan, *Mondragon: An Economic Analysis* (London: George Allen and Unwin, 1982), p.181.
7. John Jordan, *Co-operative Movement, Systems, and Futures* CFDPWP no.2 (Saskatoon: Cooperative College of Canada, 1981), p.7.
8. Harry Viteles, *A History of the Co-operative Movement in Israel* Vol.2 (London: Vallentine and Mitchell, 1967), p.643.
9. Michel Chevalier, *The Real Co-operative Challenge* CFDPWP No.7 (Saskatoon: Coop College of Canada, 1982), pp.17 and 20.
10. Richard Endress, "Types of Liminality" *American Benedictine Review*, 26:2, June 1975, p.150.
11. Paula Rayman, *The Kibbutz Community and Nation Building* (Princeton, N.J. Princeton University Press, 1981), p.250.
12. Harvey Cox, *Religion in the Secular City: Toward a Postmodern Theology* (New York: Simon and Schuster, 1984), p.130.
13. Ibid., p.126.
14. William H. Friedland et al., *Revolutionary Theory* (Allanhead, Osmun, n.d.), p.163.

INDEX

THE COMING OF WORLD WAR III

by
Dimitrios I. Roussopoulos

"In this timely book Dimitrios Roussopoulos faces a fear that is rapidly becoming in all our minds a certainty we dare not admit — the coming of World War III. The only way to defuse the certainty is by mass popular action on a larger scale than ever before so that at least we can add an 'unless' to the phrase, 'The war **will** *happen'."*

George Woodcock

"The Coming of World War III is perhaps the most provocative, thoughtful, and important book on the nuclear issue of this decade. It is indispensable reading for all peace activists and thoughtful people generally who are concerned with the future of our planet and our freedom."

Murray Bookchin

*"***The Coming of World War III** *by Dimitrios Roussopoulos is the companion volume to the fascinating book this leading Montréal radical activist edited recently under the title* **Our Generation Against Nuclear War.** *Like C. Wright Mills' prophetic best-seller,* **The Causes of World War III,** *published 25 years ago, this important new book awarns us of the imminent danger of a nuclear war of world-wide proportions.... For those who feel that the threat of an all-out nuclear war is fast becoming the major issue of the 1980's, this important book will be a useful tool that will help them oppose and reverse the fatal trend towards the total destruction of planet Earth. This is a thought-provoking book that deserves to be read and acted upon by all those who care about the future of the biosphere, and of mankind in particular. It presents an objective and realistic picture of the present situation,*

**More
books
from
BLACK
ROSE
BOOKS**

and a non-sectarian progressive view of some of the means that should be used to avoid the worst."

Dr. Jean-Guy Vaillancourt
Université de Montréal

"Dimitrios Roussopoulos has written an important book on the most outstanding question before us, namely the utter destruction of life and culture. The sheer waste of economic resources in the present international arms build-up, as manifested by the rivalry between power centres, must be stopped."

Dr. Jorge Niosi
Université du Québec

After working with the disarmament movement for more than 20 years, and having just completed a thorough investigation of the intensified arms race and the emergence of the new disarmament movements in Europe and North America, Dimitrios Roussopoulos believes a third world war *will* happen, because not enough is being done to prevent it. This conclusion has a number of radical implications for activists in the peace movement, sympathizers to its aims and those interested in social change.

This timely volume not only provides a succinct analysis of the various forces worldwide which bring us ever closer to nuclear annihilation, it also takes the reader on a tour of the numerous anti-nuclear and disarmament organizations which are working toward peace and raises a myriad of political issues which contribute to international tension.

The author offers a sympathetic yet critical analysis of the movement — country by country — in a last-ditch attempt to make both activists and the public see the issues clearly and to prevent a third world war.

Send for complete free catalogue

3981 boul. St-Laurent
Montréal, Québec
H2W 1Y5

250 pages
Paperback ISBN: 0-920057-02-0 $14.95
Hardcover ISBN: 0-920057-03-9 $25.95
International Politics/Sociology

THE FRENCH LEFT

A History and Overview

by Arthur Hirsh

"Hirsh's work is...of greatest interest..."
Canadian Journal of Political Science

"...Hirsh's (book) is an important contribution to the study of this process of political renewal, providing a clear yet sophisticated analysis of the development of its theoretical and ideological roots..."
Book Review Annual

Consisting of a new evaluation of the intellectual history of the contemporary Left in France, this book is an important contribution to understanding the debates that have had an international influence.

The work of Henri Lefevre, Cornelius Castoriadis, André Gorz, Jean-Paul Sartre, Louis Althusser, Simone de Beauvoir, Nicos Poulantzas, and other outstanding theorists are presented in separate chapters and their contributions assessed within the context of Eurocommunism, the crisis of Marxism and contemporary social movements.

253 pages
Paperback ISBN: 0-919619-23-6 $9.95
Hardcover ISBN: 0-919619-24-4 $19.95
History/Philosophy/Politics

SERVICES AND CIRCUSES

Community and the Welfare State

by Frédéric Lesemann

"One of the first to identify and re-evaluate technocratic rationality, Lesemann's book is already a classic. A warning to us all!"
David Woodsworth,
School of Social Work, McGill University

The Quiet Revolution turned on its head Québec's entire health and welfare system. Suddenly an immense government bureaucracy took over services traditionally administered by the Church and local voluntary organizations.

Services and Circuses is the long-awaited translation of Frédéric Lesemann's unique examination of the shift in Québec from clerical petit bourgeois control to bureaucratic state welfarism. The analysis is enriched and guided by the author's concern for the autonomy of local groups in the face of increased state control in all areas of life.

Québec underwent these changes extremely rapidly and therefore provides an ideal case study of a society in transition. However, Lesemann's account of the competing groups and ideologies which shaped these fundamental changes will be essential reading for all Canadians affected by the general shifting of control in our society.

Prof. Lesemann teaches social work at the Université de Montréal.

276 pages
Paperback ISBN: 0-920057-05-5 $12.95
Hardcover ISBN: 0-920057-06-3 $22.95
Social Work/Sociology

THE POLITICS OF HUMAN SERVICES

Radical Alternatives to the Welfare State

by Steven Wineman

This book is a devastating critique of the conservative and liberal policies affecting the poor and powerless as well as a personal/political account of Wineman's experiences as a worker for the welfare state. Wineman integrates human services into a resurgent radical movement that encompasses the struggles of women, people of colour, gays and lesbians, the young and old, and poor and working-class people.

While critics of the status quo often fail to move beyond rhetoric to real, workable proposals for change, Wineman is explicit and concrete, proposing a strategy that he calls radical decentralization. This strategy is concerned with not only materially supporting people who depend on the welfare state for subsistence or psychological support, but also with worker-controlled non-profit businesses; socially owned, cooperatively managed housing; participatory health care; and social support networks.

Wineman concludes with a vision of a movement, itself radically decentralized, which prefigures a new society where people are neither oppressors nor oppressed.

250 pages
Paperback ISBN: 0-920057-43-8 $14.95
Hardcover ISBN: 0-920057-42-X $24.95
Social Work/Sociology/Politics

THE ANARCHIST COLLECTIVES

Workers' Self-Management in
Spain 1936-39

edited by Sam Dolgoff

*"Although there is a vast literature on the
Spanish Civil War, this is the first book in
English that is devoted to the experiments in
workers' self-management, both urban and
rural, which constituted one of the most remarkable social revolutions in modern
history."*

Prof. Paul Avrich, Princeton University

*"The eyewitness reports and commentary
presented in this highly important study reveal
a very different understanding of the nature
of socialism and the means for achieving it."*
Prof. Noam Chomsky, M.I.T.

194 pages, illustrated
Paperback ISBN: 0-919618-20-0 $12.95
Hardcover ISBN: 0-919618-21-9 $25.95
History/Labour/Economics